Advanced Design Techniques(ADT)

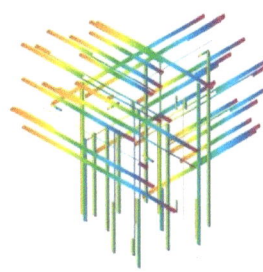

"A designer knows he has achieved perfection not when there is nothing left to add, but when there is nothing left to take away."

Antoine de Saint-Exupéry

Author:

JOHNSON WONG VOON PING

Year Published: 2017
First Edition

Praise for *ADT*

A very practical book with many useful tips. The topic on Content Research Tactics is particularly detailed, informative and nicely reinforced with practical search exercises. The topic on Infographics gives many great ideas on how presentations can be made more visually appealing within the context of the content being covered. Another interesting feature is the "Your Thoughts" page at the end of each section, which does help one do a little more thinking about what was covered.

Associate Professor Goh Wooi Boon
Associate Chair (Faculty), School of Computer Science and Engineering, Nanyang Technological University

This book has given me fresh insight and definitely improved my productivity. The information is simple to grasp and it is immediately applicable and useful to anyone regardless of their job. I would think this would be a quintessential resource for many Adult Educators out there looking for new and innovative ways to improve their practice.

Mark Nivan Singh
Deputy Director, Singapore Polytechnic

As a busy learning designer, I find that the handbook has helped me to maintain all the essential tools and techniques in one easy-referenced compendium for me to be productive in actual learning design work. The guide also serves as a thought provoking manual to try out relatively new tools such as infographic and interactive learning experience. With this guide as catalyst, I have been challenged to explore further new learning design tools. I like to recommend this guide to all learning designers to keep it as a constant companion in their professional learning design work.

Victor Kow
Principal Consultant, Victor Kow Training and Consultancy

Advanced Design Techniques(ADT)

Preface

The inception of any course design that is engaging stems from not only presenting the accurate content but also the approach to delivering a high-quality presentation of the materials, including the relevant resources in a coherent and with a *designerly* appeal to the reader.

Adopting a 'story telling' technique to unravel the subject is increasingly popular in corporate learning and development. The value of storytelling can be adopted in most parts of designing effective content to present and engage the reader.

While it is not the intent of this guide to demonstrate key elements of storytelling, the anchoring principles should take into consideration of such approach to be embedded in your designing of content materials that best fit the reader's needs.

I hope that this guide can equip you with a levelled technique that helps you in the design of any content material or resources.

Johnson Wong

Content

	Page
Preface	1
Overview	3
Topic 1 : Instructional Design and Courseware Development	4
Topic 2 : Content Research Tactics	19
Topic 3 : Referencing	45
Topic 4 : The Learner Guide – Design & Formatting Strategy	60
Topic 5 : Using PowerPoint to Create the Learner Guide and Visuals	77
Topic 6 : Graphics and Imageries	96
Topic 7 : Infographics 101	110
Topic 8 : Transforming Static Content to Interactive Experience	137
Conclusion	163
References	164
Glossary	165

© Copyright 2017   Johnson Wong

ADT Overview

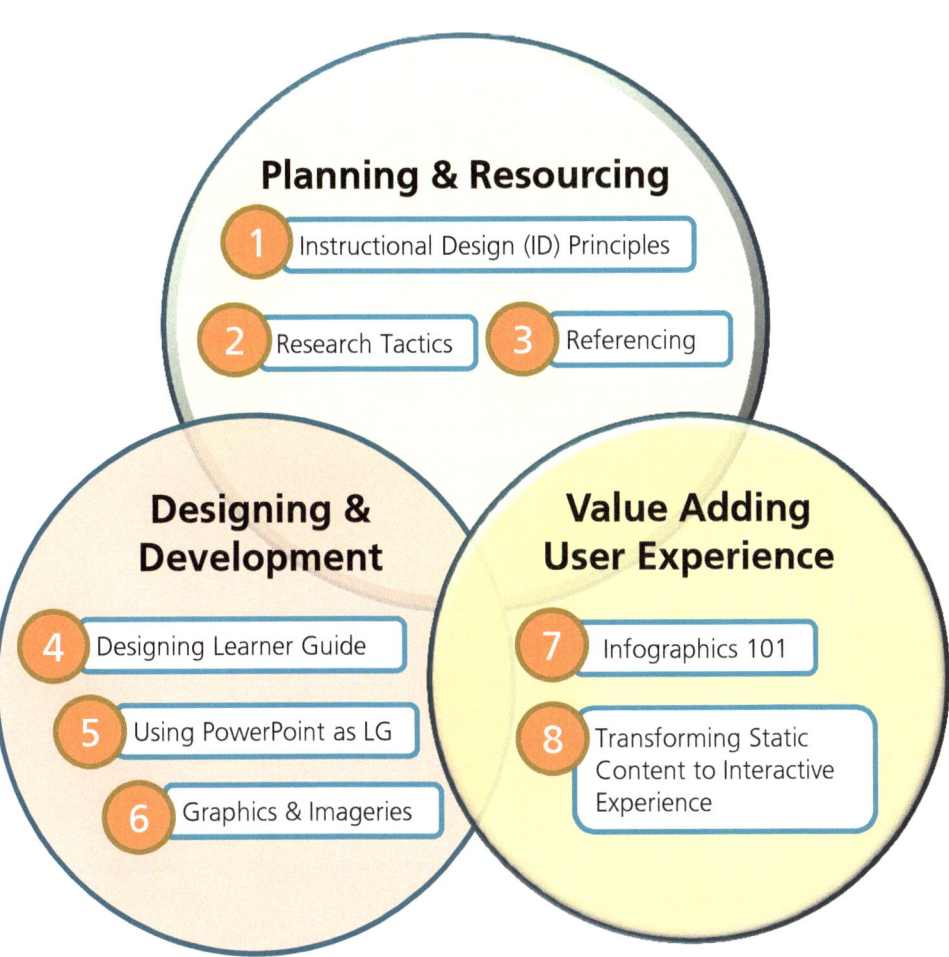

TOPIC 1
INSTRUCTIONAL DESIGN AND COURSEWARE DEVELOPMENT

- ❖ Standard Courseware Materials
- ❖ Building Learning Objectives
- ❖ Scoping and Managing Course Contents
- ❖ Sequencing Strategies
- ❖ Constructive Alignment with Assessment Goals
- ❖ Creating Relevance through Contextualisation

Topic 1: Instructional Design and Courseware Development

Introduction

Instructional design (ID) is not a linear process. It requires the designer to adopt appropriate ID strategy and use practical design techniques during the course development journey.

Revisiting instructional design

<u>Some primary considerations</u>

- ☐ Who are the learners?
- ☐ What are the desired learning outcomes?
- ☐ How will the course assess learners?
- ☐ How will the content be structured and sequenced?
- ☐ What activities are appropriate to engage the learners?
- ☐ How will the course be delivered?

> *Name the key components of a complete courseware or a full set of training materials? For example, a lesson plan.*

Topic 1: Instructional Design and Courseware Development

Standard Courseware Materials

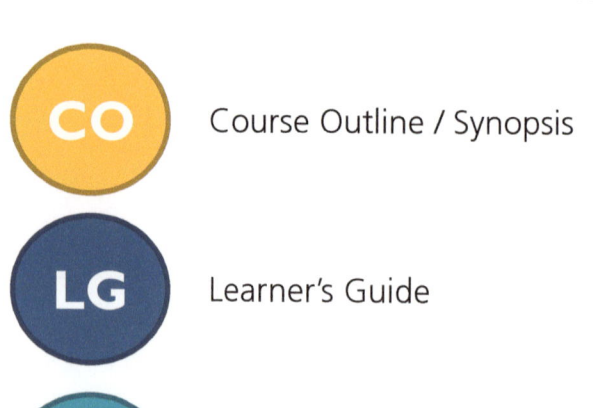 Course Outline / Synopsis

 Learner's Guide

 Lesson Plan

 PowerPoint Slides

 Trainer's Guide / Facilitator Guide

Assessment Rubric
- Optional depends on course requirements
- Could be embedded in TG.

Topic 1: Instructional Design and Courseware Development

Courseware Materials

Your Thoughts

> What are some differences between the courseware components that you have used in the past and the ones stated on the preceding page (page 6)?

'All of us must cross the line between ignorance and insight many times before we truly understand". – David Hawkins

Topic 1: Instructional Design and Courseware Development

Building Learning Objectives

- 2 main types: Terminal and Enabling Learning Objectives
- States what learners do to demonstrate that they have learnt
- Learning objectives should contain characteristics:
  - Performance standards, criteria, conditions
  - Specific, Measureable, Achievable, Relevant, Time-bounded (SMART)
- Learning objective constructed with action verbs from Bloom's 3 domains – Cognitive, Affective and Psychomotor

Practice

Revisit on – create learning objectives

Example

At the end of the program, learners should be able to <u>demonstrate</u> **qualities of a service professional when delivering go-the-extra-mile service (GEMS) to customers.**

Was the mentioned example a TLO, have PCC, and is SMART? And which Bloom's learning domain used?

How do you create a learning objective?
Use the following table as a guide this activity. You may use the design tool - "Objectives Construction Wheel' during this exercise.

State your learning objectives here	TLO / ELO (tick)		PCC / SMART (tick)		Domain and levels of Bloom's taxonomy	
	TLO	ELO	PCC	SMART	C	Level:
					A	Level:
					P	Level:

Design Tool – 'Objectives Construction Wheel' (OCW)

You can download the online template for making the *OCW* at:
https://johnsonwongvp.wordpress.com/objectives-construction-wheel-ocw-kit/

Password: ADT

Topic 1: Instructional Design and Courseware Development

Building Learning Objectives

Your Thoughts

> What are some other factors that you will consider when creating learning objectives?

Topic 1: Instructional Design and Courseware Development

Scoping and Managing Course Contents

- Factors influencing the course content scoping
    - Background information related or indirectly linked to the subject
    - Graduate profile (learning outcomes)
    - Entry requirements
    - Learner profile
    - ID model used
    - Sequencing approach to content building
    - Assessment strategy, plan

- Managing course contents

    Systematic approach with appropriate ID method used (e.g. ADDIE)
    - Learning objectives
    - Learning activities
    - Assessment methodology
    - Continuous validating the constructive alignment the preceding elements of the courseware

Topic 1: Instructional Design and Courseware Development

Scoping and Managing Course Contents

Your Thoughts

> *What are some factors influence the scoping of any course content?*

"I strive for two things in design: simplicity and clarity. Great design is born of those two things." – Lindon Leader

Topic 1: Instructional Design and Courseware Development

Sequencing Strategies

Chronological	Content arranged in time sequence or order of events. Past to present to future. (e.g. Anthropology studies, natural history)
Topical	By topics: They may be related but in no specific order. (e.g. Technology, Finance)
Whole-to-Part	Presents overarching system /model of the topics on what learner should know, then drill down to the various specific topics.
Part-to-Whole	Learners are introduced to portions of an entire subject or piece of work; where only at the end, the entire subject are presented as a whole.
Known to Unknown	Building on topics familiar to learners and leading them to what they do not know.
Unknown to Known	Deliberately put learners out of comfort zones to face an unfamiliar context/ situation. Aimed to motivate learners by showing them they need to learn more. (e.g. soft skills, physical training, boot camp.)
Step by Step	Content structure based on the steps of a task/job, or a series of cognitive process to learn a skill. (e.g. Operating a machine, closing a transaction)
General to Specific	Beginning from basic and core topics and then progress to specializes in-depth and specific ones. (e.g. IT, education)

Topic 1: Instructional Design and Courseware Development

Constructive Alignment Between Learning Objective, Activities and Assessment Goals

Constructive alignment is the means to ensure that the courseware is designed so that the learning outcomes, the delivery and assessment strategies and content are consistent to enable the learners to achieve the targeted competencies. This alignment process begins with the end in mind.

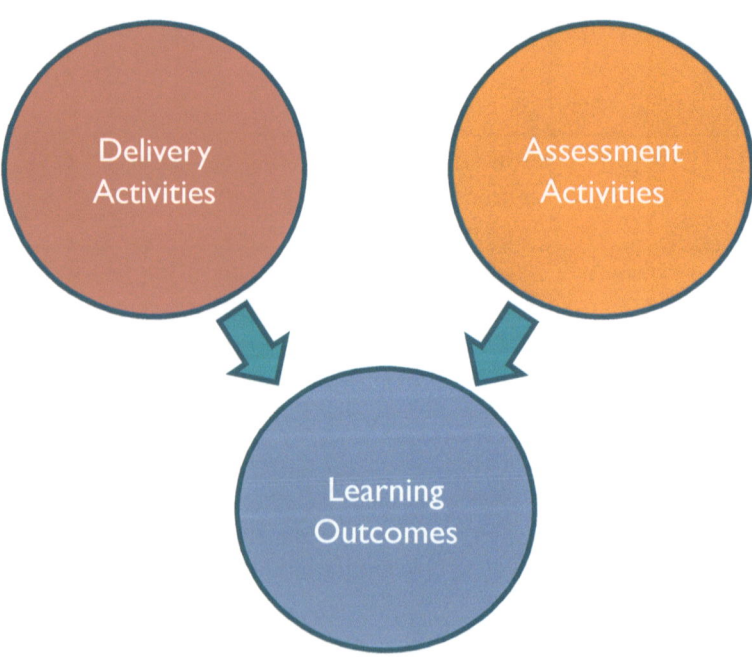

Topic 1: Instructional Design and Courseware Development

Constructive Alignment Between Learning Objective, Activities & Assessment Goals

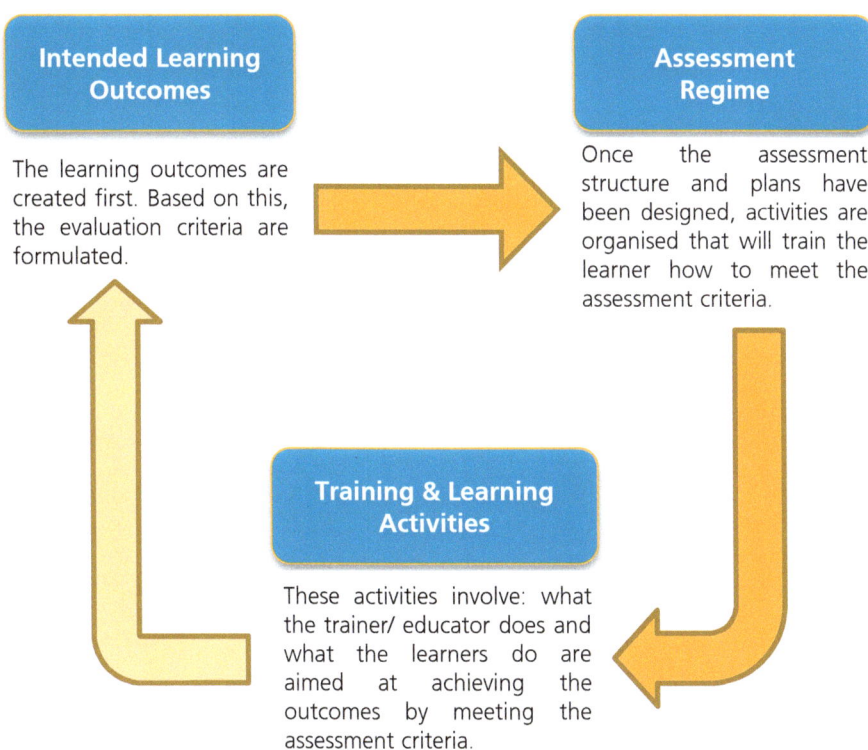

A Model of Aligned Curriculum

Intended Learning Outcomes

The learning outcomes are created first. Based on this, the evaluation criteria are formulated.

Assessment Regime

Once the assessment structure and plans have been designed, activities are organised that will train the learner how to meet the assessment criteria.

Training & Learning Activities

These activities involve: what the trainer/ educator does and what the learners do are aimed at achieving the outcomes by meeting the assessment criteria.

Topic 1: Instructional Design and Courseware Development

Constructive Alignment Between Learning Objective, Activities & Assessment Goals

Your Thoughts

> *How do you ensure constructive alignment when developing courseware?*

"When we talk about 21st century pedagogy, we have to consider many things—the objectives of education, the curriculum, how assessment strategies work, the kind of technology infrastructure involved, and how leadership and policy facilitate attaining education goals."

— Chris Dede, Harvard University

Topic 1: Instructional Design and Courseware Development

Creating Relevance through Contextualisation

- Consideration factors:
    - Address individual needs of learners
    - Industry requirements
    - Company specific requirements (workplace context)
- Contextualisation should NOT comprise assessment rigor and principles of assessment (if assessment is a requirement)
- Contextualisation should also meet regulatory and legal requirements (e.g. workplace safety)

Topic 1: Instructional Design and Courseware Development

Creating Relevance through Contextualisation

Your Thoughts

> *How do you contextualise your courseware?*

"We must teach the way students learn." – Pedro Nogeura

TOPIC 2
CONTENT RESEARCH TACTICS AND HACKS

- ❖ Content Research
- ❖ Using Google Search
- ❖ Google Scholar 101
- ❖ Use of Commercial Resources & Libraries

Topic 2: Content Research Tactics

Content Research

Before carrying out any content research, plan your search gives you more targeted and effective results. Here' are some tips:

1. List the requirements
2. Scope the topic factors
3. Define the objectives
4. Create limits /boundaries of the search process
5. Choose an approach
6. Select a user-friendly search tool
7. START search and archive (catalogue your search results)

Topic 2: Content Research Tactics

Content Research

General approaches for courseware content research

1. Interviews with subject matter expert (SME)
2. Research at libraries – book/ periodicals search
3. Corporate providers of content materials
4. Web search - use of search engines (Google, Yahoo, Bing)
5. Online libraries (public)
6. Online commercial research databases, libraries

Common e-tools for content research

1. Google search engine
2. Google Scholar
3. National Library Board's e-catalogue
4. ERIC
5. ProQuest

Topic 2: Content Research Tactics

Your Thoughts

How do you conduct research work on the content that is needed?

"To do the writing, I have to have time to do research." – Jean-Jacques Annaud

Topic 2: Content Research Tactics

Using Google Search

Why use proper search techniques?

Everyone including researchers, students, writers, content designers, etc. requires information, and they use search engines for that very reason. People spend most of their time **seeking for the right information** because they're not aware of the proper search techniques. Learning and using proper search techniques will help you in the following ways:

- Improved quality of search outcomes
- Save time

Note: Queries used and examples are included inside brackets [ ] for higher readability.

Topic 2: Content Research Tactics

Using Google Search

Basic search tips

1. Keep It Simple.

- Make your search **straightforward and web-friendly**. Start by using one or two words, and gradually adding relevant words, until you're satisfied with the results. *Less is more* for this search process; meaning the fewer words you query for, the more results the search engine provides as output.
- For example:
  - Query: [*who is the president of ABCDE*]
  - Better query: [*president of ABCDE*]

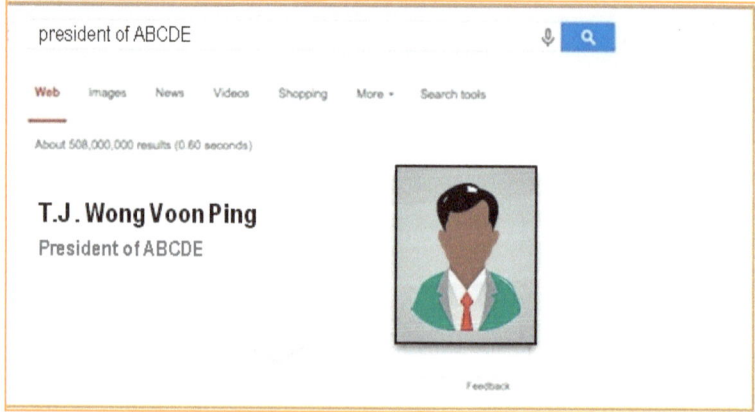

Topic 2: Content Research Tactics

Using Google Search
Basic search tips
2. Choose your words carefully
- When deciding what words to put in the search box, try to choose words that are likely to appear on the particular site that you intend to look for. For example, instead of saying **my left side of the head hurts**, say a **migraine**, because that is the word in a medical site would use.
- For example:
  - Query: [what is the route from City A to City B]
  - Better query: [City A to B route]

3. Worry less about the little things
- **Spelling.** The spell checker automatically produces the most common spelling of the given word, whether or not you spell it correctly.
- **Capitalization.** A search for **Straits Times** is the same as a search for **straits times**.

Topic 2: Content Research Tactics

Using Google Search

Basic search tips

4. Sequence of Keywords

- **Select the right keywords to do your search**. Search results entirely depend on the given keywords, and if keywords are chosen correctly, then results are more efficient.
- Place yourself in the shoes of the writer, and think of what words he/she would use to describe what you're attempting to find. If you're finding a phrase or quote, then **keep the sequence of the words as accurate as possible** to get the optimum search results.
- Examples:
  - Query: [itself divided house cannot stand]
  - Better search query: [A house divided against itself cannot stand] (part of a quote by Abraham Lincoln)

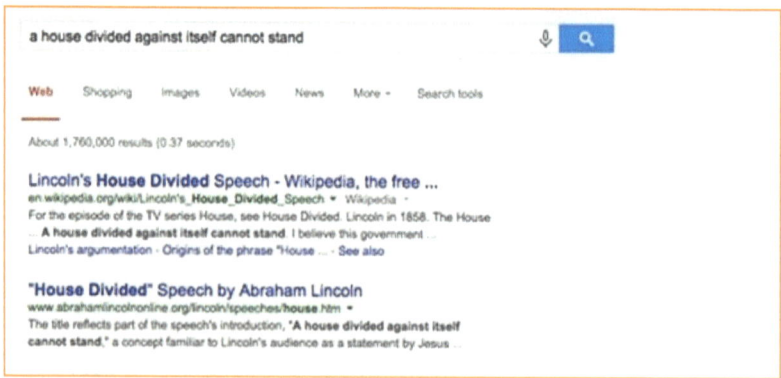

Topic 2: Content Research Tactics

Using Google Search

Basic search tips

5. Get quick answers

- For many searches, Google will do the processing for you and show a reply to your question in the search results. Some features, like information about sports teams, aren't available in all regions.

Weather	Search **weather** to see the weather in your location or add a city name, like **weather seattle**, to find weather for a certain place.
Dictionary	Put **define** in front of any word to see its definition.
Calculations	Enter a math equation like **5*9223**, or solve complex graphing equations.
Unit conversions	Enter any conversion, like **5 US dollars in Japanese Yen**
Quick facts	Search for the name of a celebrity, location, movie, or song to find related information

Topic 2: Content Research Tactics

Using Google Search
Basic search tips
6. Skip unnecessary parts

- Google **is smart enough to handle most of your typos**, and other things that could just be ignored. That's why you should skip those things in your query to save time.

- You should not worry about the following when writing a search query:
    - Spelling
    - Cases (uppercase or lowercase)
    - Punctuation (dot, question mark, exclamation mark, and more)
    - Special characters (plus, minus, brackets, and more)

Topic 2: Content Research Tactics

Using Google Search
Basic search tips
7. Social information
- Google is apt at handling searches related to people, profiles and social networks. You can **search for individuals and their social profiles** using:
    - **+[profile-name]**
    - By adding a '+' before a profile-name, you can find Google+ profiles and pages.
    - For example: [+johnson wong]

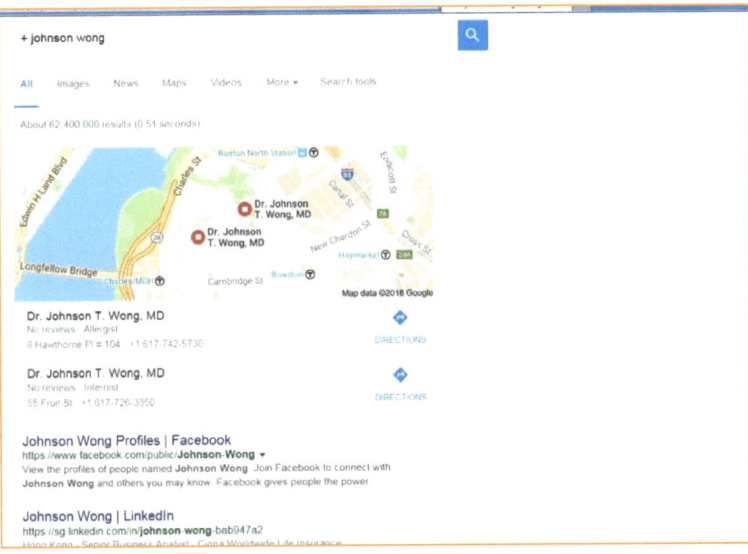

Practice

Let's do a simple online search exercise.

Hint*: Make use of the 7 basic steps to do your search.

Search for the following:

1) 2nd President of Singapore

2) Steps to administer an injection

3) International version of Harvard Business Review

4) Quotations used by Albert Einstein

5) What is the Latin translation of innovation

6) Conversion of 28 square metres into square feet

7) Search on the latest book for storytelling technique from the United States.

Topic 2: Content Research Tactics

Your Thoughts

What other approaches do you use when doing an online information search?

"To design is to communicate clearly by whatever means you can control or master."
– Milton Glaser

Topic 2: Content Research Tactics

Using Google Search

Search operators

1. Punctuation & symbols

❖ While you can use the punctuation marks below when you search, including them doesn't always improve the results. If we don't think the punctuation will give you better results, you'll see suggested results for that search without punctuation.

Symbol	How to use it
+	Search for Google+ pages or blood types Example: **+Chrome** or **AB+**
@	Find social tags Example: **@taipei101**
$	Find prices Example: **ipad $1000**
#	Find popular hashtags for trending topics Example: **#gardencity**
"	By putting a word of phrase in quotes for the search, the results will only include pages with the same words in the same order as the ones inside the quotes. Useful for looking for exact word or phrase. Example: **"advance design techniques"**
*	Add an asterisk as a placeholder for any unknown. Example: **info:google.com**
..	Separate numbers by two periods without spaces to see results that contain numbers in a range. Example: **dryer $50..$100**

Topic 2: Content Research Tactics

Using Google Search
Search operators
2. Operators

- These search operators are words that can be added to searches to help narrow down the results. You don't have to worry about remembering every operator, because you can also use the *Advanced Search* page to create these searches.

Operator	How to use it
site:	Obtain results from certain sites or domains Example: olympics site:espn.com
related:	Find sites that are similar to a web address you knew. Example: related:newsweek.com
OR	Find pages that might use one of several words. Example: marathon OR race
info:	Gather information about a web address, including the cached version of the page, similar pages, and pages that link to the site Example: info:google.com
cache:	Look at what a page looks like the last time Google visited the site. Example: cache:harvard.edu

Note: When you search using operators or punctuation marks, don't add any spaces between the operator and your search terms. A search for **site:nytimes.com** will work, but **site: nytimes.com** won't.

Topic 2: Content Research Tactics

Using Google Search
Advance Search
A. Steps for an advance search

1. Go to the Advanced Search page.
   - ❖ 'Advanced Search for websites'
   - ❖ 'Advanced Search for images'
2. In the "Find pages with" section, enter your search terms.
3. In the "Then narrow your results by" section, choose the filters you want to use. You can use one or more filters.
4. Click Advanced Search.

*You can also use the various filters in the search box with search operators to refine your search.

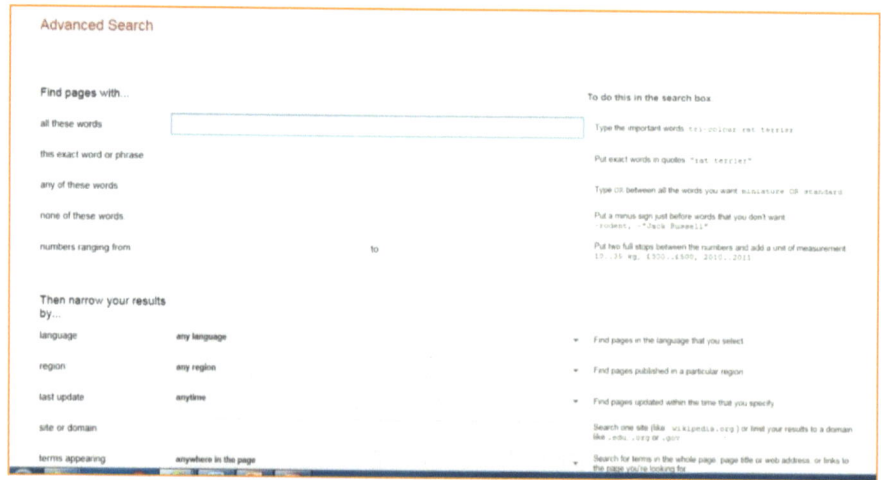

Topic 2: Content Research Tactics

Using Google Search
Advance Search
A. Steps for an advance search

Advanced Search filters to use

<u>Websites</u>
- Language
- Last updated date
- Region
- Site
- Where the search terms appear on the page
- SafeSearch
- Reading level
- File type
- Usage rights (find pages that you have permission to use)

<u>Images</u>
- Size
- Aspect ratio
- Color
- Type
- Site or domain
- Filetype
- SafeSearch
- Usage rights (find pages that you have permission to use)

Topic 2: Content Research Tactics

Using Google Search
Advance Search
B. Synonym search

- The synonym search feature finds synonyms of a specified word in the search query. This is helpful for when you want to search for a word and all its similar words without having to spend time looking for them individually.

- By means of adding the tilde symbol (~) before a word tells Google to search for the words and its synonyms too. Type your search query in the format of [~synonymWord otherWords] to search for the word and its synonyms in a single search.

- For example: [~leafy vegetable]

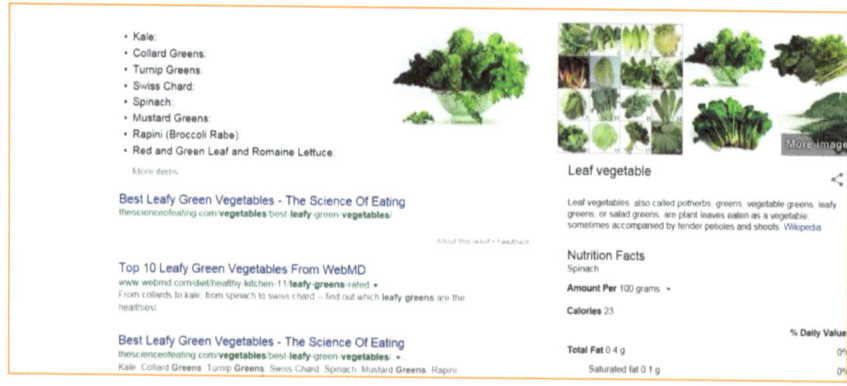

Topic 2: Content Research Tactics

Your Thoughts

How do you run an academic / professional document search?

"Research is what I'm doing when I don't know what I'm doing."
— Wernher von Braun

Topic 2: Content Research Tactics

Google Scholar 101 (Brief summary)

Google Scholar provides a simple way to search for scholarly literature. From one place, you can search across several disciplines and sources: articles, theses, books, abstracts and court opinions, from academic publishers, professional societies, online repositories, universities and other web sites.

https://scholar.google.com/

Topic 2: Content Research Tactics

Google Scholar 101 (Brief summary)
Example

 What Are You Searching?

 How Do You Google It?

author:	" "
This part will ask Google to search by Amabile rather than papers involving the word "amabile"	This part will ask Google to search for specific results, you can put the authors full name or initials in quotes.

author:amabile creativity "social psychology"

The middle part will be similar to the normal Google search.

Practice

Let's run an academic / professional document online search exercise.

Hint*: Make use of the Google Scholar to do your search.

Search for the following:

1) You have partial information of title of the journal paper: '*Training Engagement Theory*' and the first author's name is *Traci Sitzmann* , and its in '*the Journal of Management*'.

2) You have partial information of the journal paper that is: the **volume number is 51** in '*Australian Journal of Adult Learning*', the author is **Marina Falasca**.

3) You want to search for a list papers related to topic of '*Workplace based learning*' for the last 2 years.

Topic 2: Content Research Tactics

Google Scholar 101 (Brief summary)

Search Tips
Getting better answers

- If you're new to the topic, it may be useful to pick up the terms from secondary sources. E.g., a Wikipedia's site article for "overweight" might then suggest a Scholar search for "paediatric hyper alimentation".

- If the search results are too specific for your required search, find out what they are citing in their "References" sections. Referenced works are often more general in nature.

- Likewise, when the search results are too generic or basic for you, click "Cited by" to view newer papers that referenced them. These newer articles will often be more accurate.

> **Resource**
> About Google Scholar
> https://scholar.google.com.sg/intl/en/scholar/help.html#general
> How to use Google Scholar 101 :
> https://youtu.be/5AcgyzxmP2Q
> Getting the most out of Google Scholar :
> https://www.youtube.com/watch?v=jDf9IiP_9Ng

Topic 2: Content Research Tactics

Use of commercial resources libraries

Academic ~ Corporate databases/ libraries

https://www.ebsco.com/

https://www.ebscohost.com/

http://www.springer.com/gp/

http://www.proquest.com/

http://www.sciencedirect.com/

http://eric.ed.gov/

Topic 2: Content Research Tactics

Use of commercial resources libraries

Other commercial resources

http://library.elearningbrothers.com/

https://www.flickr.com/

http://www.shutterstock.com/

https://www.blendimages.com/

https://www.pond5.com/

Topic 2: Content Research Tactics

Your Thoughts

> *What have you been using (any tools/ applications/ libraries) to gather resource for subject content development?*

"Recognizing the need is the primary condition for design." – Charles Eames

TOPIC 3
REFERENCING

- ❖ Intellectual Property and Copyright
- ❖ Text Citation Standards
- ❖ Tools for Referencing and Content Source Cataloguing

Topic 3: Referencing

Intellectual Property and Copyright

Intellectual Property (IP) refers to the creations of the human minds for which exclusive rights are recognised. Innovators, artistes and business owners are granted certain exclusive rights to a variety of intangible assets for a specified duration.

~ Intellectual Property Office of Singapore (IPOS)

Types of IP
- Patent
- Trade Mark
- Registered Design
- Plant Varieties protection
- Copyright
- Layout-design of an Integrated Circuit
- Geographical Indication
- Trade Secret

Topic 3: Referencing

Intellectual Property and Copyright

Copyright protects work such as novels, computer programmes, plays, sheet music and paintings. The author of a copyrighted work has the right to reproduce, publish, communicate and adapt his work.

These exclusive rights combined as a bundle of rights that is known as copyright and gives the power for the owner to control the commercial exploitation of his work.

What is protected by Copyright?

- Literary works (e.g., written works, source codes of computer programs)
- Dramatic works (e.g.,. scripts for films and dramas)
- Musical works (e.g., melodies)
- Artistic works (e.g., paintings, photographs)
- Published editions of the above works
- Sound recordings
- Films
- Television and radio broadcasts

Topic 3: Referencing

Intellectual Property and Copyright

Assuming the copying is within permissible limits of the Copyright Act, regardless of nature of copy (e-copy/hardcopy)	
Circumstance	Action required
1. Copy article for personal use – to read, but <u>not to share</u>.	No action required
2. Pass a link for article to friends/colleagues (for the other parties to access directly)	
3. Download article to computer and distribute to friends/colleagues via email.	*Considered Copying.*
4. Download article and post it on portals, website, course materials etc	

Source:
COMPASS
      http://www.compass.org.sg/cIndex40.aspx
IPOS
      http://www.ipos.gov.sg/

Topic 3: Referencing

Intellectual Property and Copyright

Terms of Protection

Type	Duration
Literary, dramatic, musical and artistic works	70 years from the end of the year in which the author died. Specifically for photographs, or if the work is published after the death of the author, it lasts for 70 years, from the end of the year in which the work was first published.
Published editions of literary, dramatic, musical or artistic works (layout)	25 years from the end of the year in which the edition was first published.
Sound recordings and films	70 years from the end of the year in which the sound recording or film was first published.
Broadcasts and cable programmes	50 years from the end of the year of making the broadcast or cable programme.
Performances	70 years from the end of the year of the performance.

Adapted from: https://www.nla.gov.au/how-long-does-copyright-last

Practice

Intellectual Property and Copyright

Consider the following points:

1. How is the type of materials in your courseware development is subjected to this IP and copyright? Why?

2. During the design of content, how do you ensure that you're adhering to the IP and Copyrights?

3. Draw a mind map of IP and Copyright reference to content development work. (include digital, web, or traditional communication platforms)

Topic 3: Referencing

Intellectual Property and Copyright

Your Thoughts

> *What is the relationship between plagiarism and copyright?*

"An original writer is not one who imitates nobody, but one whom nobody can imitate." – François-René de Chateaubriand

Topic 3: Referencing

Text Citation Standards

Your Thoughts

How do you cite text in your courseware?

Topic 3: Referencing

Text Citation Standards

- **American Psychological Association (APA) Style**
    - Resource site from APA: http://www.apastyle.org/

- **Harvard Reference Style**
    - Here is a useful referencing tool: http://www.harvardgenerator.com/
    - Resource sites from Imperial College, United Kingdom ; and University of Western Australia:
    - http://www.otago.ac.nz/library/pdf/Harvard_referencing.pdf
    - http://guides.is.uwa.edu.au/ld.php?content_id=15709737

Other referencing styles :
http://www.wales.ac.uk/en/OnlineLibrary/StudySkills/ReferenceStyles.aspx?tab=tab2

Topic 3: Referencing

Text Citation – General information

- Author-date method of citation allows the reader to recognize the source of research. The reason is the author's or authors' surname and the year of publication are placed in the text of the report or article.

- In quotations, you need to state the specific page number of the work you have cited, together with the author and year of publication.

- At the end of the essay or research report, all citations are listed in the alphabetical reference sequence.

- The following are two general formats to reference citations in- text:

    1. Citation is incorporated into the text. In this case, the author's surname appears as part of the narrative. Only the year of publication is typed in brackets. An example:

    > Amabile (1996) point out that creativity in the context...

    2. The citation is inserted within brackets. Author surname and publication year placed in brackets. An example:

    > Creativity is defined as the generation of ideas products that are *novel* and *useful* (Amabile, 1996).

Adapted from:
www.johnwiley.com.au/highered/psych2e/jcu_demo/interactive_writing/dswmed

Practice

Let's do a simple referencing exercise.

Hint*: Choose the right standard and style for making citation.

Part One – In-Text citation

<u>Edit the following for the citation of a reference in text:</u>

From the examples below, identify the correct form of citation:

    a. According to McGriffs (1988), math ability is acquired.

    b. Individual differences in memory have been found (Guildford, 1987).

    c. In 1998, Savange found that young woman respond to self-worth dilemmas differently than men.

    d. Lavin (1986) observed that TV serves as a surrogate parent for some teenagers. He found that "drama addicts" have limited parental contact.

    e. All of the above are correct

Resources - In-Text Citation Practice
http://www2.elc.polyu.edu.hk/cill/exercises/intextrefs.htm#q1
http://www.johnwiley.com.au/highered/psych2e/jcu_demo/interactive_writing/dswmedia/referencelist/ref.htm

Practice

Let's do a simple referencing exercise.

Hint*: Choose the right standard and style for making citation.

Part Two – Writing a reference list (APA format)

There is at least one mistake in every entry. Correct them and check your answers.

1. Brett, P. 1994. A genre analysis of the results sections of sociology articles. English for Specific Purposes, 13, 47-59.

Bridgeman, B., & Carlson, S. B. Survey of academic writing tasks. Written Communication, 1, 247-280.

Campbell, A. F. (1983). Organise your English. London: Hodder and Stoughton.

Clyne, M. (1983). Culture and discourse structure. In Smith L. E.(Ed.), Readings in English as an international language (pp. 163-167). London: Prentice Hall.

Dudley-Evans, A. (1984). "A preliminary investigation of the writing of dissertation titles". In G.
    James (Ed.), The ESP classroom: Methodology, materials and expectations (pp. 40-46). Exeter: University of Exeter.

Cookson, L. (1984). Writing. London: Hutchinson.

Resources - Writing a reference list
http://www2.elc.polyu.edu.hk/cill/exercises/intextrefs.htm#q1

Topic 3: Referencing

Tools for Referencing and Content Source Cataloguing

Zotero is an open-source reference management software to organize bibliographic data and related research materials (such as PDF files).

Main features include web browser integration, online syncing, generation of in-text citations, footnotes and bibliographies, as well as integration with the word processors Microsoft Word, LibreOffice, OpenOffice.org Writer.

Source:
https://www.zotero.org/

Topic 3: Referencing

Tools for Referencing and Content Source Cataloguing

Your Thoughts

> *How do you catalogue your content materials (for referencing)?*

"Clutter is a failure of design, not an attribute of information."
— Edward Tufte, Statistician and Professor

Topic 3: Referencing

Knowing what can be use and reference them correctly:

© Copyrighted materials in PPT slides

- ❖ <u>Refrain</u> from embedding videos/using screenshots of Article
    → This is considered a copy if slides were distributed to learners.

- ✓ Strongly recommended to <u>Use Hyperlinks</u> to access videos and materials online.
- ✓ Include <u>in-text citation</u>
    - ✓ Link to google image (if image is to be used)
    - ✓ Link to article available on the web
- ✓ <u>Provide references</u> on the last page of the document.

TOPIC 4
THE LEARNER GUIDE DESIGN & FORMATTING STRATEGY

- ❖ Strategy for Design and Formats
- ❖ Learner Guide Formats
- ❖ Page Layouts
- ❖ Use of 'White Spaces'
- ❖ Font Types and Sizes
- ❖ Typography
- ❖ Headings, Numbering
- ❖ Icons/ Symbols
- ❖ Readability
- ❖ Summaries
- ❖ Glossary, Marginal Notes

Topic 4: The Learner Guide – Design and Formatting Strategy

Strategy for Design and Formats

A relational overview

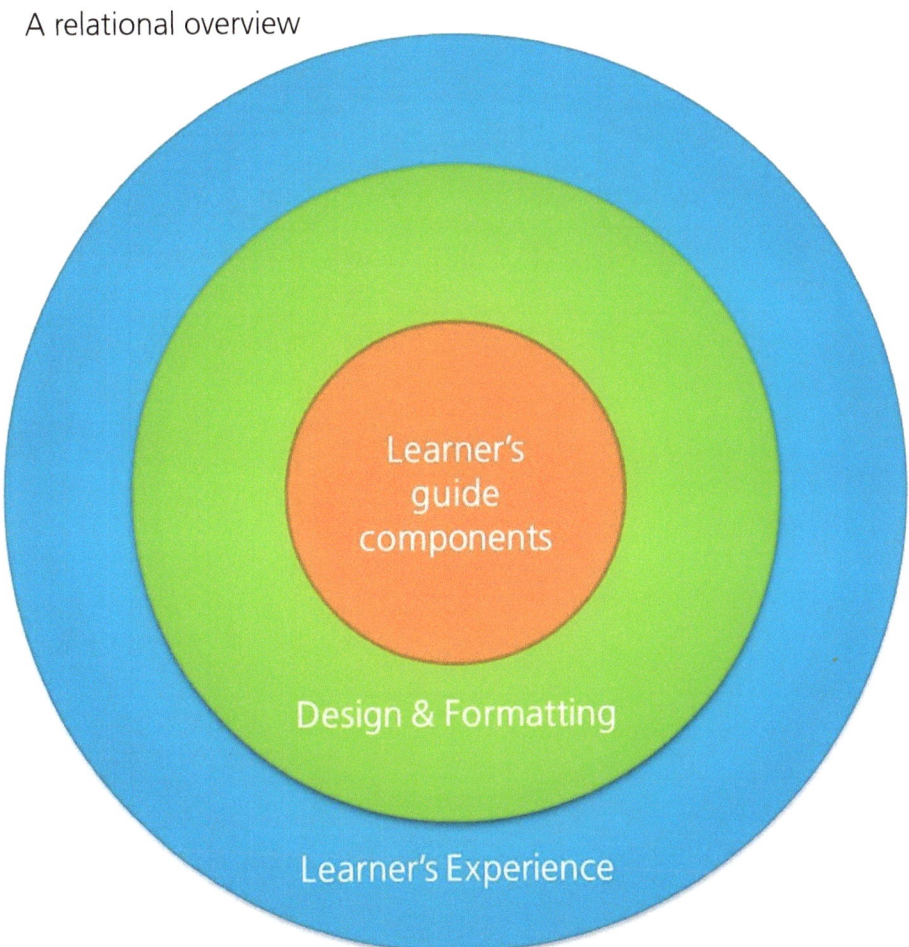

The design and formatting bridges the learning components and the learner's experience. If you have a poor design, it will certainly impact the way the learner perceives the learning experience.

Topic 4: The Learner Guide – Design and Formatting Strategy

Learner Guide Formats

10 Typical learner's guide (LG) components are:

1.	Cover Page	Title and packaging of the LG
2.	Blank Page / Version Control	Blank or versions documentation
3.	Table of Contents	List of subject topics and others
4.	Introduction Page / Preface / Executive Summary	Provides an overview of the programme/ course materials
5.	Navigation / Directions Page	Provides instructional guide on how to use the LG
6.	Topics - Objectives - Headings - Subject content - Graphics, Imageries, Charts, Diagrams - Activity - Review Page	Main content - Learning outcomes - Subject content - Illustrations - Practice / Exercises / Learning Activities - Summary review on each topic learnt
7.	Conclusion	Summaries the main take away of the programme/ course.
8.	References / Bibliography	Listing of cited works, referenced sources.
9.	Glossary / Index	List of terms and abbreviations used with explanations. List of words/ phrases and associated pointers with corresponding page numbers.
10.	Appendices	Learning resources – Worksheets, Checklists, Charts.

Topic 4: The Learner Guide – Design and Formatting Strategy

Page Layouts

Good layout of the page aids learners by:
- ✓ Make the text easier to read
- ✓ Provide a consistent pattern throughout the entire LG
- ✓ Emphasis on relevant and essential facts (alignment to topic's learning objectives)
- ✓ Guide reader through entire information blocks
- ✓ Organises blocks of information
- ✓ Facilitates quick scanning and retrieval of information

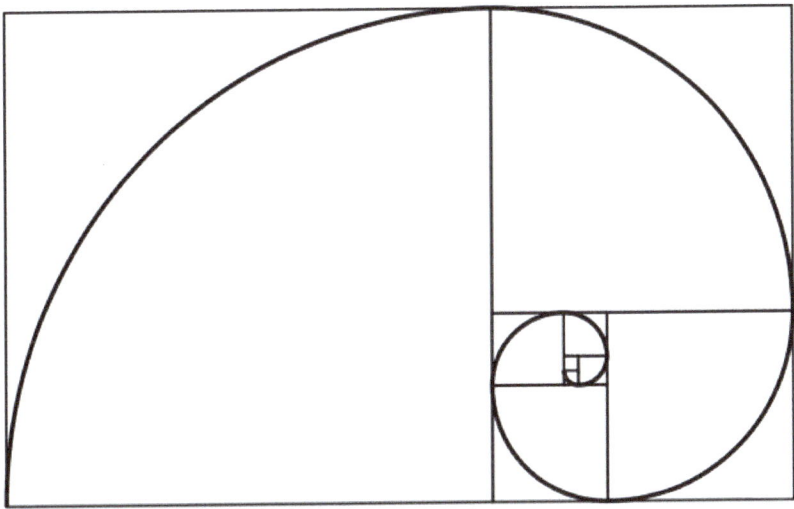

The use of golden ratio (1.61803398875) in your page layout can provide a better visual appeal and proportion for your reader.

Topic 4: The Learner Guide – Design and Formatting Strategy

Use of "White Spaces"

Learning materials should be easy to read, and the use of 'white spaces' can achieve this. Without an adequate amount of 'white spaces', the text becomes harder to read, graphics will lose their emphasis, and the balance of the elements in the page will be disrupted.

'White space' also commonly known as 'negative or blank space'. It can mean the areas such as borders, margins, gaps between paragraphs, etc. Too little and too much of 'white spaces' will affect the page's composition.

Here's an excellent infographic on reasons to use 'White Space'.

Topic 4: The Learner Guide – Design and Formatting Strategy

Font Types and Sizes

Font type is the basic building block of any printed page. It is not uncommon for beginner designer to use multiple fonts for a document. While it is recommended to use a maximum of two or three fonts for a single document, there are situations when it is necessary to use more. In that case, how often and why should always be at the forefront of designers mind. Fonts may come in italic, bold, light, weighted, expanded, or condensed versions.

For instructional materials, use a font in the 12-point range, although titles, heading, and even subheadings should be larger. Different fonts have different associations. Imagining looking at the menu of an expensive, upper-class restaurant. You probably would visualize it using the old European font. On the contrast, the menu of a new and funky restaurant. You will likely to have pictured a decorative font for the header and a sans serif font for the text.

Resource site :
http://blog.presentationload.com/tips-for-selecting-fonts-and-text-layouts/

Topic 4: The Learner Guide – Design and Formatting Strategy

Font Types and Sizes

Font Type Category	Description and example
Oldstyle	Oldstyle is designed to similarly as Roman inscriptions. This font is commonly found in the body text of most books. It is pleasing to the eye and easy to read. e.g. Goudy, Garamond, Times New Roman
Modern	Modern is created to look more mechanical compared to Oldstyle. The modern style has been around since 17th century, so it is not all that modern by today's standards. e.g. Bodoni, Ultra, Walboum
Slab serif	Slab serif is another variation from Modern that is designed to be more attractive to the eye. One can quickly relate this type of font to those posters about 'Wild West Wanted'. e.g. New Century Schoolbook
Script	Script is a fancy and elegant font. It mimics the cursive handwriting style. e.g. Bickley, Vivaldi
Decorative	Decorative fonts set the tone of a playful and light-hearted mood. e.g. Hollyweird, Curlz MT

Topic 4: The Learner Guide – Design and Formatting Strategy

Font Types and Sizes

Font type can have three types of relationships

1. Concordant – When one type family is often used without significant variety in style, size, weight, etc. The effect is harmonious, quiet, sedate and formal.

2. Conflicting – When you combine typefaces that are similar in style, size and weight. This similarity conflicts because the type is not the same (concordant), nor is it different (contrasting).

3. Contrasting – When you combine separate typefaces and elements that are clearly distinct from each other. Most designs that attract attention have a lot of contrast embedded, and these differences are usually greatly emphasized.

Can you identify the following images which is concordant, conflicting or contrasting?

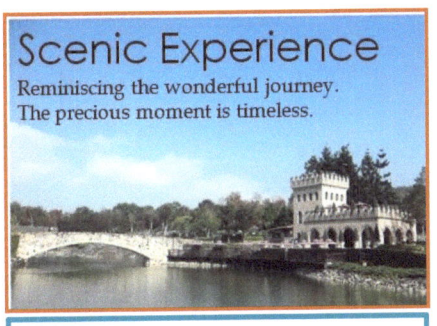 

Topic 4: The Learner Guide – Design and Formatting Strategy

Typography

Typography the art and science of arranging type to make written language legible, readable and appealing when displayed. The arrangement of type involves selecting typefaces, point sizes, line lengths, line spacing (leading), and letter-spacing (tracking), and adjusting the space between pairs of letters (kerning). Also, the term typography is applied to the style, arrangement, and appearance of the letters, numbers, and symbols created by the process.

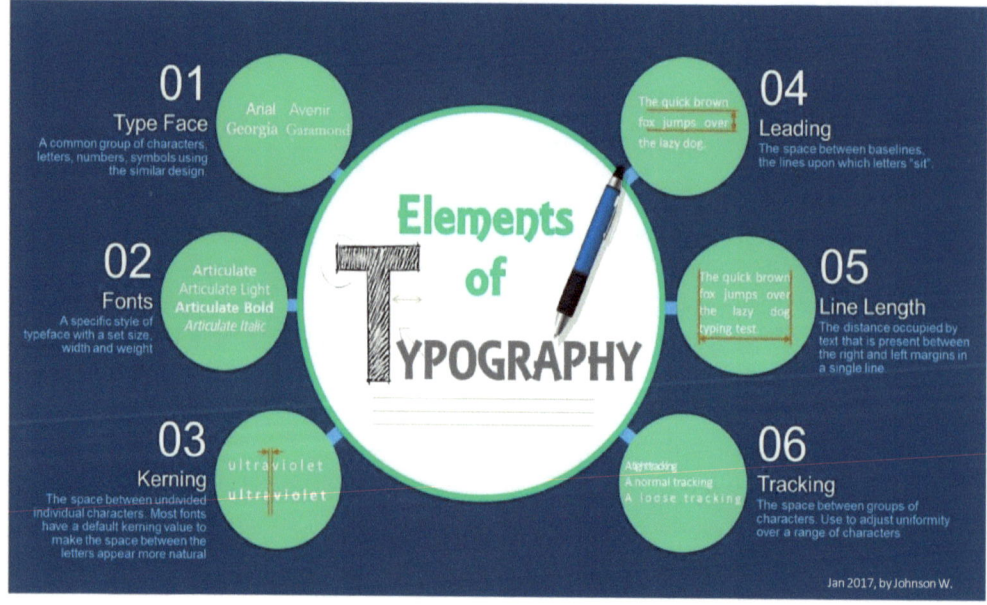

Topic 4: The Learner Guide – Design and Formatting Strategy

Fonts Types and Sizes

Your Thoughts

Readability of content – how do you design for this?

"Most people think typography is about fonts. Most designers think typography is about fonts. Typography is more than that, it's expressing language through type. Placement, composition, typechoice."

- Mark Boulton

Topic 4: The Learner Guide – Design and Formatting Strategy

Headings

Headings and Sub-headings help readers orientate to the learning material quickly. When moving on to write a new section, always give it a title. Headings and sub-headings break up the contents and provide the learner with immediate focus. It also guides the learner in his or her learning and allows them to pause their reading appropriately.

2.1 AaB	2.1 AaB	1.1.1.1 A	1.1.1.1.1	1.1.1.1.1	1.1.1.1.1.	1.1.1.1.1.	1.1.1.1.1.
Heading 1...	Heading 2...	Heading 4	Heading 5	Heading 6	Heading 7	Heading 8	Heading 9

Styles

Numbering

A numbering system can be used to organize topics or pointers. Care should be taken in order not to confuse readers. For example, a unit divided into Sections 1, 2 and 3 and further subdivided into Sections 1.1, 1.2, Sections 2.1, 2.2 or Sections 3.1 and 3.2. Arabic numerals are a better choice over Roman numerals for such sequencing.

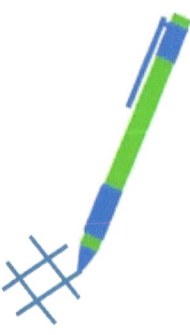

Topic 4: The Learner Guide – Design and Formatting Strategy

Readability

It is the ease with which a reader can understand a written text. Readability of the document depends on its content and typography. The success of it depends on the extent to which the reader can comprehend it, read it at optimum speed and find it interesting.

The Linsear Write Formula

This readability index helps ensure the use of short, concise sentences that reduce reading and comprehension time. To measure readability:

1. Pick any 100-word sample
2. Count all (1) syllable words in your sample except for 'the', 'is', 'are', 'was' and 'were'. Assign 1 point for each.
3. Count the number of sentence in the 100-word sample to the nearest period or semicolon. Assign 3 points for each.
4. Add the count of all the one syllable words and the sentences to get the total score.

> e.g. A 100 word sample has 58 one-syllable words and 6 sentences.
> $58 ÷ (6 × 3) = 76.$
> This is a Linsear rating of 76.

Scores	Interpretation
70 to 80 points	Average learner reading level
80 points	Close to ideal
Above 80 points	Too simple
Below 70 points	Too complicated

Practice

Let's do a simple formatting exercise.

Hint*: Use the basic principles of formatting – layouts, typography, headings and other design elements..

Choose a half page newspaper article (opinions / focus/ review)

Type the content in your computer application and add your reflections about (review).
Use one of the approaches mentioned to create a 1-page layout of the chosen content.

Get someone to comment on your design layout of the content material based on the principles learnt.

After that, refine and improve your design based on the feedback given.

Topic 4: The Learner Guide – Design and Formatting Strategy

Icons/ Symbols

Visual signs, symbols and icons attract the reader and cue them to the task or activity required to be done. They should be used consistently throughout the learner guide for them to be effective.

Topic 4: The Learner Guide – Design and Formatting Strategy

Summaries

Summaries at the end of each topic give a section or unit closure of information and allow the learner to have remembered the relevant facts easily as it highlights the key concepts and information of that part.

Topic 4: The Learner Guide – Design and Formatting Strategy

Glossary / Indexes

A glossary is a list of terms in a particular domain of knowledge with the definitions for those terms. Traditionally, a glossary appears at the end of a book and includes terms within that book which are either newly introduced or at least uncommon.

Marginal Notes

These are notes that appear in the margins of a page. They may be essential information, a summary of key facts, the definition of words or phrases, statistics, quotations, case studies, etc. They can captivate reader's immediate attention and provide focus to a topic at a glance.

Topic 4: The Learner Guide – Design and Formatting Strategy

Design and Formatting

Your Thoughts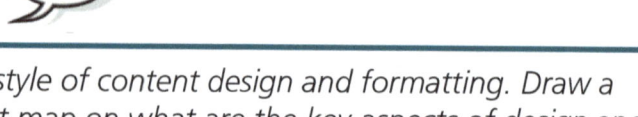

Develop your style of content design and formatting. Draw a simple concept map on what are the key aspects of design and format of your work.

"Visual organization is the deliberate prioritization of meaning within a visual design. It's the process of applying the principles behind perception - how we make sense of what we see - to illuminate relationships between content and actions. "   – Luke Wroblewski

TOPIC 5
USING POWERPOINT TO CREATE LEARNER GUIDE & VISUALS

- ❖ PowerPoint over Microsoft Word
- ❖ PowerPoint Tips
- ❖ Use of Themes and Libraries
- ❖ Creating Diagrams and PowerPoint

Topic 5: Using PowerPoint to Create Learner Guide & Visuals

MS PowerPoint Over MS Word

Advantages of PowerPoint over MS Word:

- ✓ Able to cater for revision of content by 'slide-based', that is the pagination will not run when new content is needed to be updated.
- ✓ Orientation content in slides format means that it can be easily transferred to or fro from topic to topic without messing up the entire learning document.
- ✓ Formatting consistency can be governed and designed easily by using slide master options (will discuss this in more detail later)
- ✓ Editing and working with imageries and diagrams in the PowerPoint environment is more user-friendly
- ✓ Additional notes can be hidden (for facilitator / trainer notes)
- ✓ Content (such as learner guide) can be easily converted for presentation purposes.
- ✓ Multimedia elements can be easily added (Audio / Video)
- ✓ Ease of conversion to more interactive document or for e-learning.

Topic 5: Using PowerPoint to Create Learner Guide & Visuals

MS PowerPoint Over MS Word

Your Thoughts

> *What is your preferred authoring tool for creating learner guides? And why?*

"I am always doing that which I cannot do, in order that I may learn how to do it." — Pablo Picasso

Topic 5: Using PowerPoint to Create Learner Guide & Visuals

Use of Styles, Slide Master and Shortcuts

> ➢ Use 'Slide Master' to create consistent styles for fonts to be use – headers, body text, points, sub-points.
> ➢ Choose a suitable font type and sizing.
> ➢ You can use the standard set of layouts in the 'Slide Master' or edit according to your requirements
> ➢ Adopt the tips of visual communication when selecting the type of styling that suits the content & structure.

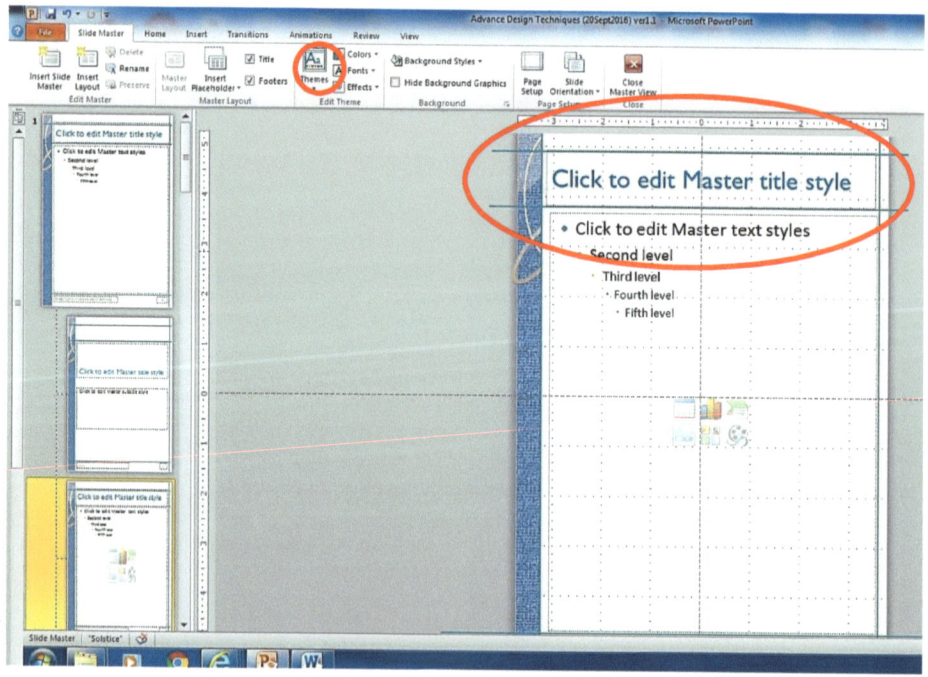

Topic 5: Using PowerPoint to Create Learner Guide & Visuals

PowerPoint Tips - Visual Communications

General

Skip the stock template slide theme

Limit bullet points less than 7

Choose your fonts and colours carefully

Use high-quality image and graphics

Use appropriate charts that illustrate your 'story'

Use video/ audio when appropriate (show concrete examples)

Use animation with a purpose (including transitions across slides)

Topic 5: Using PowerPoint to Create Learner Guide & Visuals

Using PowerPoint

Your Thoughts

> *List your steps in planning and creating content if you are using PowerPoint or Word.*

"Plans are nothing; planning is everything." – Dwight D. Eisenhower

Topic 5: Using PowerPoint to Create Learner Guide & Visuals

PowerPoint Tips - Visual Communications

Decide on a design 'theme'.
Recommend to create your own design theme

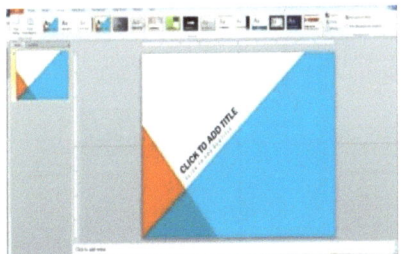 

PowerPoint Theme   Custom Design Theme

Recommendation: Don't use more than 7 lines of text per slide

Topic 5: Using PowerPoint to Create Learner Guide & Visuals

PowerPoint Tips - Visual Communications

Choose appropriate fonts

Choose easy to read fonts

Topic 5: Using PowerPoint to Create Learner Guide & Visuals

PowerPoint Tips - Visual Communications

Topic 5: Using PowerPoint to Create Learner Guide & Visuals

PowerPoint Tips - Visual Communications

Select good contrast between text and background

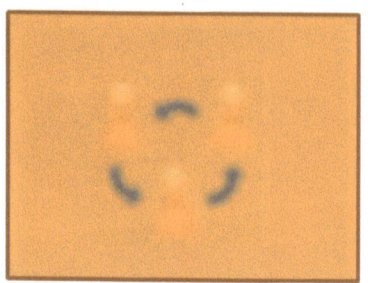 

Choose appropriate colours

© Copyright 2017 Johnson Wong

Topic 5: Using PowerPoint to Create Learner Guide & Visuals

PowerPoint Tips - Visual Communications

Use text colours that are contrasting to draw attention

Your content is important.
Often it's easy to miss the point.

Use high quality image and graphics

© Copyright 2017 Johnson Wong

Topic 5: Using PowerPoint to Create Learner Guide & Visuals

Use of Themes and Libraries

> You can also select a background design from 'Themes' in the tab or create your design.

> There are online libraries (commercial or non-profit organisations) that provide ready to use design templates.

> Commercial application such as 'Grammarly' enables learning designers to do grammar checks of their content materials. (https://www.grammarly.com)

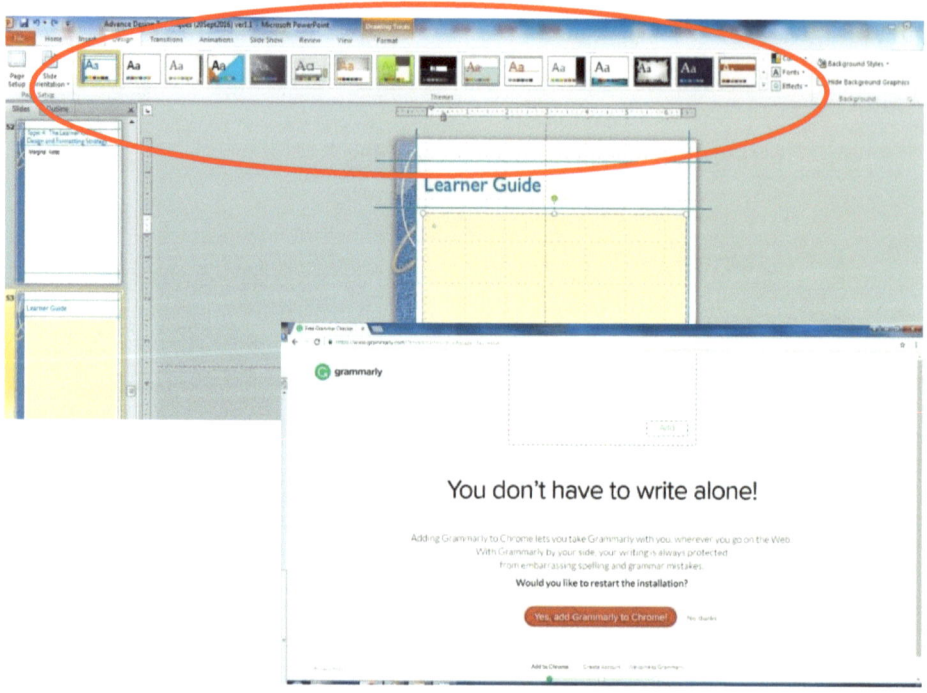

Topic 5: Using PowerPoint to Create Learner Guide & Visuals

Creating Diagrams with PowerPoint

- Conceptualize the diagram that you wish to create.
- 'Shapes', 'SmartArt' and 'Charts' to create the diagrams or figures that are basic and easy to use.
- In the 'Format' tab you can edit and change the shapes of the elements that you've created.

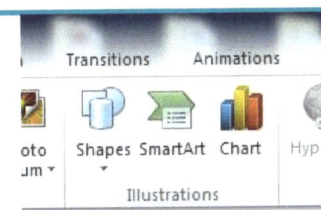

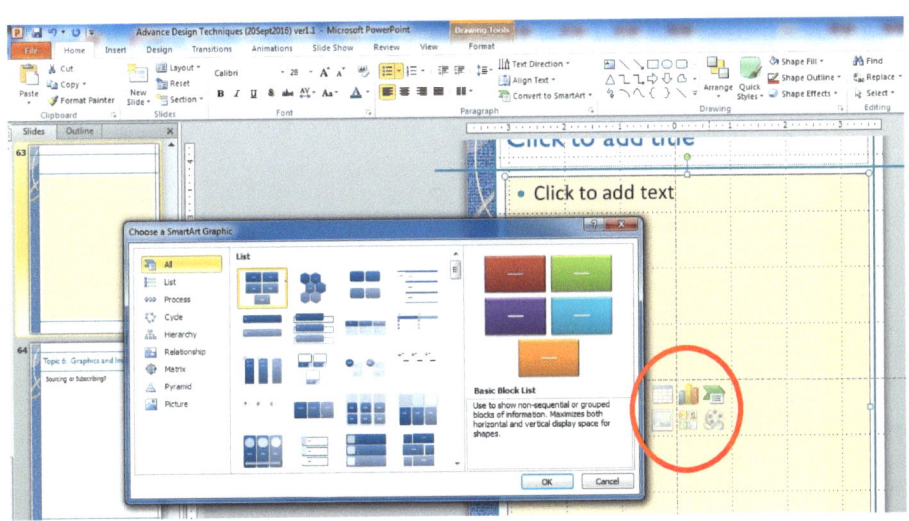

Topic 5: Using PowerPoint to Create Learner Guide & Visuals

Creating Diagrams with PowerPoint

General Tips
Formatting an image / clipart from external source
- Select the image and the 'Format' Tab will appear.
- Click the 'Color' icon, click and go to the 'Set Transparent Color'.
- An icon will appear, go and click on the area that you want to make transparent.

Removing the 'white' background in Picture A.

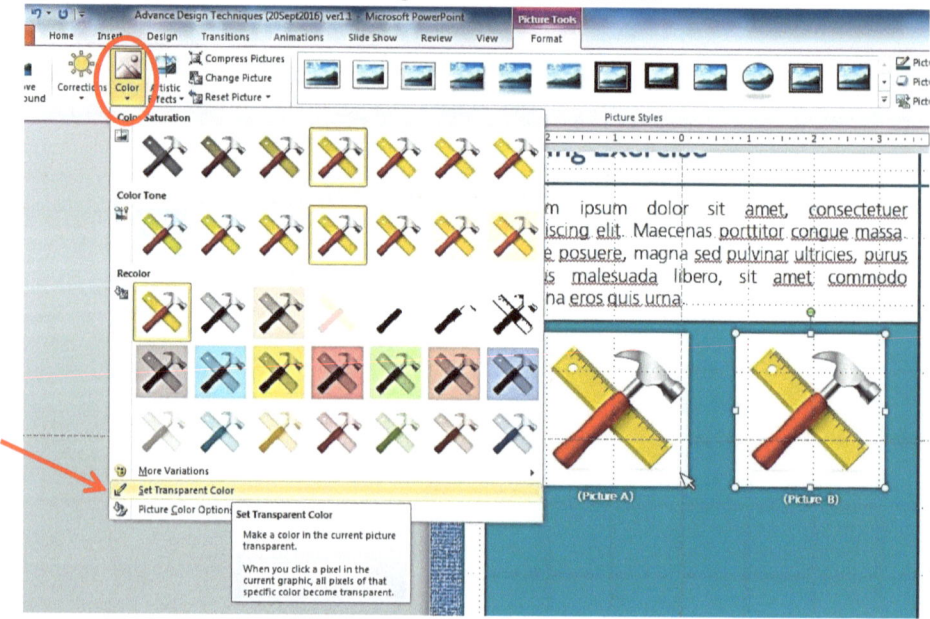

Topic 5: Using PowerPoint to Create Learner Guide & Visuals

Creating Diagrams with PowerPoint

General Tips

Aligning Shapes and Textboxes

- Select the shapes or textboxes that you wanted to create alignment.
- Go to the 'Format' tab, select 'Align' dropdown button, options of alignment will be shown. Make your selection for the alignment style.

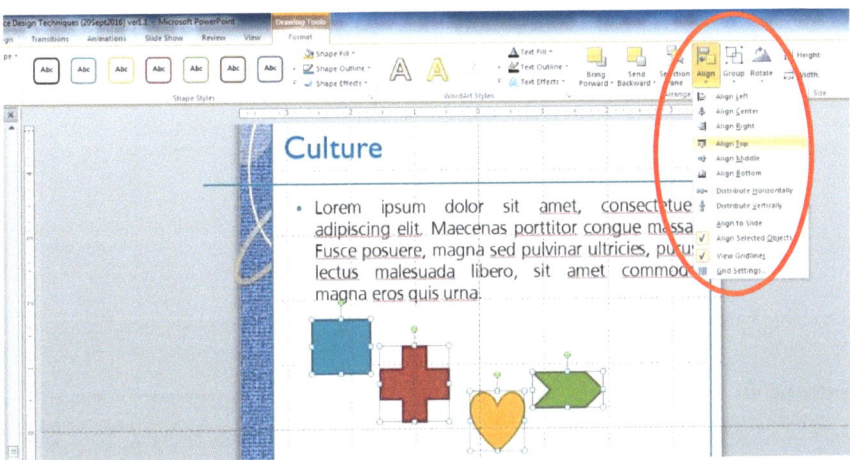

Topic 5: Using PowerPoint to Create Learner Guide & Visuals

Creating Diagrams with PowerPoint

General Tips

Merge Shapes (for PowerPoint 2013 and later versions)

- Select the shapes that you wanted to merge or modify.

- Customize a pre-existing shape, by merging two into one. Select both shapes by holding down Ctrl and clicking. Then, beneath the Format tab, click Merge Shapes near the top left. Click Union to make the two shapes one.

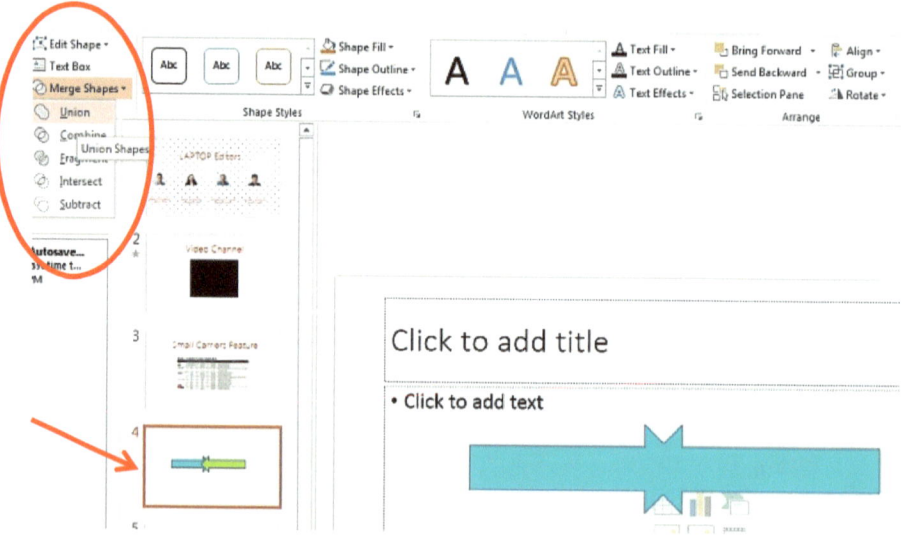

Topic 5: Using PowerPoint to Create Learner Guide & Visuals

Creating Diagrams with PowerPoint

General Tips

Merge Shapes (for PowerPoint 2013 and later versions)

- Click Combine to make one shape with the overlapping part of the shapes omitted.

- There are other options such as 'Fragment', 'Intersect' or 'Subtract' you can choose depending on your requirement.

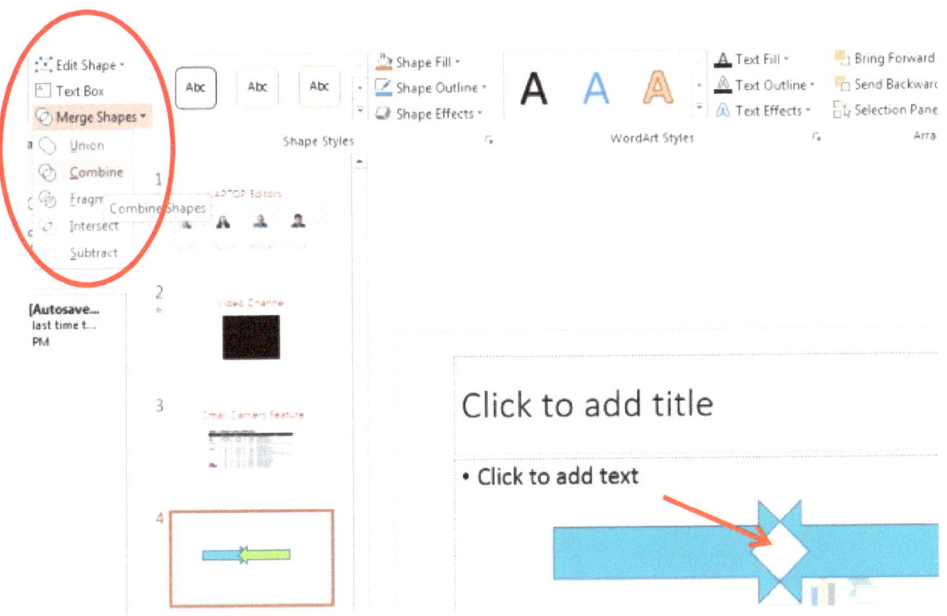

Practice

Let's create a simple LG PPT topic.

Hint*: Use the principles and techniques covered in the earlier sections to work on this exercise.

Your task is to create a **single topic** using PPT for the following information given:

Scan the QR codes:

QR Code 1: Use this to select the appropriate text information in several abstracts given.

Password : adt01

QR Code 2: Use this to the relevant image resource given.

Password : im01

Topic 5: Using PowerPoint to Create Learner Guide & Visuals

Creating Diagrams with PowerPoint

Your Thoughts

> *What are some other ways you can design and create diagrams with PowerPoint?*

"Design is the intermediary between information and understanding."
— Richard Grefé

TOPIC 6
GRAPHICS AND IMAGERIES

- ❖ Sourcing or Subscribing
- ❖ Intellectual Property, Creative Rights and Royalty free
- ❖ Create User-Friendly Graphs and Imageries

Topic 6: Graphics and Imageries

Sourcing or Subscribing?

Depending on your requirements and budgetary constraints, there's no perfect solution for obtaining graphics and imageries for your ID work or visual or marketing projects.

Sourcing for 'Free' images and illustrations
Here are some references to begin with:

Free vector art from:
https://www.vecteezy.com

Free graphic resource from:
http://www.freepik.com/

Free photos from Flickr → Use Creative Commons Option
https://www.flickr.com/search/?q=creative%20commons

Topic 6: Graphics and Imageries

Sourcing or Subscribing?

<u>Other Free resources:</u>

FREE ICONS WITH COMMERCIAL USAGE RIGHTS
https://www.smashingmagazine.com/tag/freebies/
http://www.iconarchive.com/commercialfree.html
http://www.flaticon.com (needs attribution)
http://graphicburger.com/
http://www.softicons.com/commercial-icons
http://www.vectorian.net/free-vintage-vectors.html

FREE VECTORS WITH COMMERCIAL USAGE RIGHTS
http://www.vectorportal.com
https://openclipart.org

Alternative approach
Create your database of graphics, images, photos, etc.
- Take your photographs / stills
- Make your compilation
- Draw sketches of ideas and document them digitally

Topic 6: Graphics and Imageries

Sourcing or Subscribing?

Subscribing

There are numerous sites that provide subscription-based service with large databases for stock images, graphics, illustrations, customizable clipart based on monthly or annually subscription model.

Shutterstock
http://www.shutterstock.com/

Adobe Stock:
https://stock.adobe.com/

PresenterMedia
http://www.presentermedia.com/

gettyimages
http://www.gettyimages.com/

Topic 6: Graphics and Imageries

Sourcing or Subscribing?

Recommendation – Combination Strategy
- A mixed approach to adopting 'free' resources and subscribing service from at least one of the provider will provide a steady stream of resources needed for your projects throughout the year.

Your Thoughts

What is your approach to sourcing for images?

Practice

Let's do a sourcing for images exercise

Hint*: Use the recommended sites that to source for images.

Select theme / subject for collecting the graphics / images:
e.g. Hobby, Travel, Home and other subject matter of preferences

Next, use the recommended sites to source for the desired images. Collect as many as possible and do a collage of what fits your theme most suitable.

Present them in a layout of preference and write annotations where you have sourced them from.

Practice keeping an archive of graphics and images in a catalogue manner as this will enable you to locate and re-use them when needed in future quickly.

Topic 6: Graphics and Imageries

Intellectual Property, Creative Rights, Royalty-free?

In Topic 3, we have covered parts for intellectual property (IP) and copyright rights on written and published materials in depth.
Here, the focus is on 'IP' and 'Creative Rights' for imagery, illustrations and graphics used when we are developing materials for ID or marketing projects or presentation visuals.

Intellectual property (IP) refers to creations of the intellect for which a monopoly is assigned to designated owners by law. Intellectual property rights (IPRs) are the protections granted to the creators of IP and include trademarks, copyright, patents, industrial design rights, and in some jurisdictions trade secrets. Artistic works including music and literature, as well as discoveries, inventions, words, phrases, symbols, and designs, can all be protected as intellectual property.

Topic 6: Graphics and Imageries

Intellectual Property, Creative Rights, Royalty-free?

Creative Commons

One category to consider for searching quality assets that you can use commercially (or non-commercially) is "Creative Commons," which has recently become popular.

The intention behind Creative Commons is to provide sharing of works with the online community without a price but requires attribution to the original creator.

Most of Creative Commons assets only require that you attribute the creator when you use their work. However, there are varying sub-categories that define what you can and can't do with their asset.

Discover more about how Creative Commons works and about its sub-categories with these clarifying infographics on the next page.

Topic 6: Graphics and Imageries

Intellectual Property, Creative Rights, Royalty-free?

Creative Commons License
Some rights reserved

- CC licenses caters for a more flexible management of rights
- Gives creators the ability to select the types of protections that govern the use of their work.

Attribution
Person(s) may copy, distribute, display, perform the work and make derivative works and remixes based on it only if they give the licensor the credits (attribution).

Non-commercial
Person(s) may copy, distribute, display and perform the work and make derivative works and remixes on it for non-commercial purposes.

Share-alike
Person(s) can distribute derivative works only under a license identical to the license that governs the original work.

No Derivative
Person(s) can only copy, distribute, display or perform verbatim copies of the work, not derivative works and remixes based on it.

For more information, visit the **Creative Commons** at : https://creativecommons.org/

Topic 6: Graphics and Imageries

Intellectual Property, Creative Rights, Royalty-free?

Royalty Free

It should be noted that "Royalty Free" assets still predominantly fall under the "Copyright" category as they are not in the open-source domain. Often, a misconception is that "Royalty Free" means that the asset is free, and this is not true. Generally, you pay a one-time fee or subscription fee to obtain access to the asset to use it.

For "Royalty Free" assets, you can use them commercially however you'd like without having to pay royalties to the owner. Hence, if you are searching for graphics or other assets that you can use commercially or make a profit, then you would want to find royalty free assets. Importantly, even after you have paid for royalty free assets, the owner still retains the copyright.

Topic 6: Graphics and Imageries

Intellectual Property, Creative Rights, Royalty-free?

Your Thoughts

> *What is your current practice for sourcing graphics and images?*
>
> *How do you protect the work that you have created (diagrams, charts, graphics)?*

"If I had asked people what they wanted, they would have said faster horses."
— Henry Ford

Topic 6: Graphics and Imageries

Creating User-Friendly Graphics and Imageries

Some useful applications with user-friendly interfaces for creating impactful graphics, visuals and presentation materials are:

- Canva (online graphic design platform)
- Pikotchart (web-based infographic application)
- Pixlr (cloud-based set of image tools and utilities)
- Sketch Book Pro (drawing app and painting software)
- Google Drawing(web-based diagramming software)
- Google Sketchup (3D modeling software)

Topic 6: Graphics and Imageries

Creating User-Friendly Graphics and Imageries

Tips on selecting and using these tools?

1. Decide what your requirements on usage for creating quick, easy and impactful graphics are.

2. Advise to try out at least 2 of the applications mentioned on the preceding page (Canva or Pixlr or Google Drawing, etc.) and two that you have searched on the internet (https://techreviewpro.com/best-free-graphic-design-software-create-stunning-graphics-4976/)

3. Test them by doing

   a) a simple sketch of an idea with simple annotations

   b) a simple flow chart sketch with an image added.

4. Make your comparisons of the usability and time taken for completed

5. Lastly, once you have made your selection; practice, practice, practice and you'll be on your way to mastery.

Practice

Let's create a simple diagram / graphic

Hint*: Use tips on selecting and using the tools mentioned in the preceding page.

Choose your favorite topic
List the elements that you require in the design diagram / graphic. Make sure it is logically ordered and relevant design elements included.

Create the half page (A4) graphic / diagram.

Get someone to comment on your design and improve it. Reflect on what item(s) are missing or needs to be refined. Do make a note to remember when you are creating the similar graphic/ diagram.

TOPIC 7
INFOGRAPHICS 101

- ❖ What is Infographics and reason to use infographics?
- ❖ Why Is It Useful For Instructional Design (ID)?
- ❖ Principles of Infographics
- ❖ How Can We Create Engaging Infographics?
- ❖ When to Use Infographics?
- ❖ Tools Available
- ❖ Invaluable Resources and Hacks

Topic 7: Infographics 101

What is infographics?

Infographics are a visually compelling communication medium that done well can communicate complex data in a visual format that is potentially viral. They take rich and complex data and present them in a visual shorthand.

Infographics are one efficient way of combining the best of text, images and design to represent complex data that tells a story in a cohesive and impactful manner.

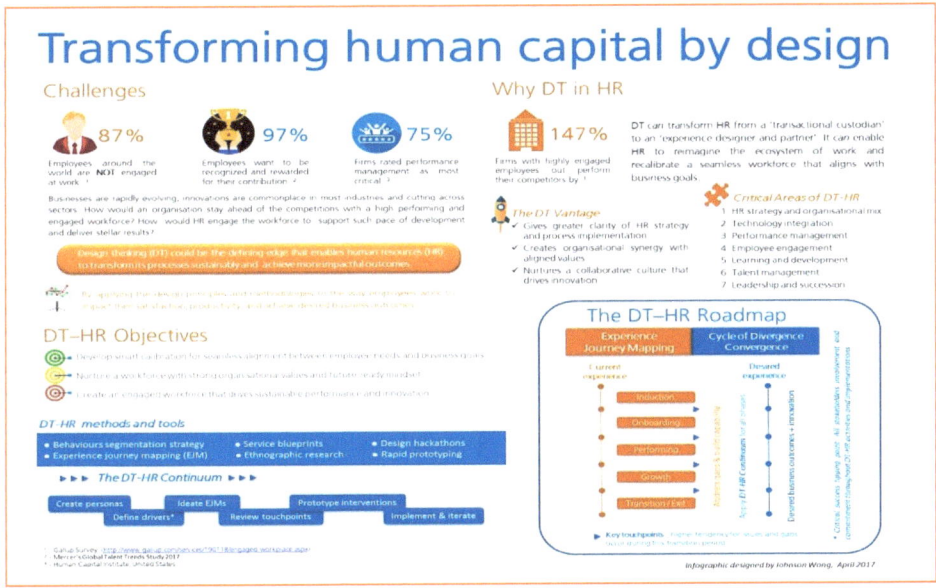

There are a lot of reasons to choose infographics, but the main argument is this: Infographics are visual items, and humans are 'visually wired' creatures. In fact, 90% of the information transmitted to your brain is visual.

Topic 7: Infographics 101

Reasons to use infographics?
Infographics are:

1. Easily scanned and viewed
Most people are highly visual, and because 90% of the information that comes to the brain is visual you need to tap into that "ocular nerve."

2. Compelling and eye-catching
People love facts, figures and statistics. Use some compelling images and graphics and "voila", you have addictive content!

3. Viral capabilities
Due to infographics attractiveness, the capacity for them to be shared on social networks and become viral is much higher than normal text content.

4. Global reach
Infographics can provide the across the cyberspace with global coverage where local print media could achieve.

5. Shows an expert knowledge and insight of a topic
The knowledge and skills required to design the infographic will demonstrate your competence as an expert in the field or subject.

Topic 7: Infographics 101

Infographics for ID

Your Thoughts

What will be some reasons for you to use infographics in your instructional design work?

"The soul never thinks without an image." – Aristotle

Topic 7: Infographics 101

Why is it Useful for ID?

✓ When it comes to instructional design particularly heavy content (data, concepts, calculations, charts, etc.), the infographic is a useful component to encapsulate the entire learning 'chapter / topic' and serves as an effective take away of the lesson.

✓ It can be used to introduce new and complex issues in any subject matter.

✓ It provides the instructional designer with an alternative in creating more engaging content that is more appealing.

✓ It creates a clear flow of information and increases the retention of learning.

✓ It serves as visual element that can be contextualized to tell a story or process that leads to more insightful learning.

Topic 7: Infographics 101

Principles of Infographics

Some basic principles of infographics
1. Appeals to wider audience
2. Visual potency
3. Relevance
4. Clear and succinct
5. Ability to 'go viral'
6. Simplifies complex ideas
7. Animate raw data

Some best practices when designing infographics
1.. Communicate ONE central idea
2. Communicate the data clearly
3. Layering – Must See, Can See and Should See
4. Make it easy to navigate
5. Keep it beautiful

Topic 7: Infographics 101

When to Use Infographics?

If you wonder when to create an infographic, take a moment and ask yourself three questions.

1. **Is there data available?**
   - Excellent infographics have lots of information. The graphics itself helps illustrate the points that the data is making.

Stating 8 out of 10 or looking at the above image, which is more compelling?

   - However data isn't enough – there needs to be enough data, and of a compelling nature to make the graphic effective. *Does the data have statistical significance?* If not, an infographic is premature.

Topic 7: Infographics 101

When to Use Infographics?

2. **Is written form of information hard to understand?**
   - Infographics are excellent for communicating information that is difficult to digest in writing. The use of charts and tables are a better way to illustrate the information with greater clarity than writing out the numerical data of a study.

   Building a timeline can create a visual reference for time and history – visual resumes are a great example of this in use.

3. **How many infographics have you been using?**
   - Try to making the visuals interesting. Use a wider variety of medium to communicate the content. If you've completed many infographics in the past, try something different.
   - If infographics are the only approach for communicating the content, it may be time to evaluate whether other content forms are to be avoided.

Topic 7: Infographics 101

How Can We Create Engaging Infographics?

Value-centric visuals

Powerful visuals provide the unique dimensions to communicate and illuminate insights. Here's a simple analogy for building insights when designing meaningful visuals.

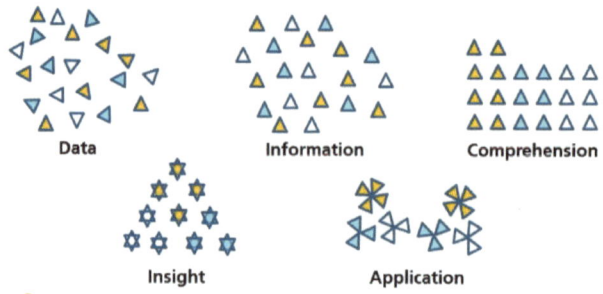

Alignment of values, organization components, people and processes need to be embedded seamlessly in any value-centric communication.

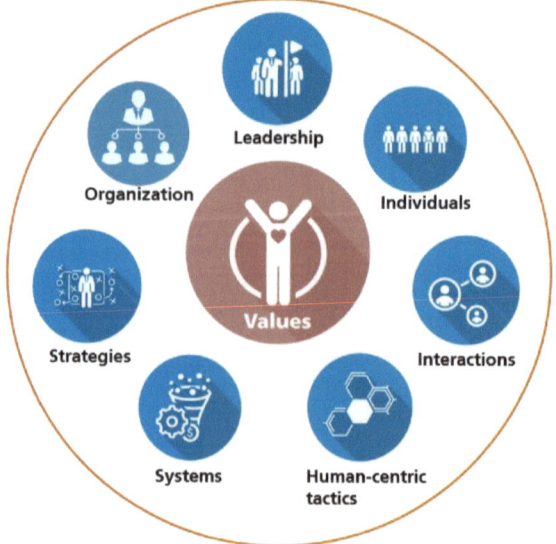

Topic 7: Infographics 101

How Can We Create Engaging Infographics?

Steps to creating infographics
1. Choose a story for the infographic
2. Select a type of infographic
3. Gather the relevant data
4. Design the infographic
5. Integrate into your ID work

> *Key questions you have to ask:*
> What should your infographic be showing?
> What is the core idea or message you want to deliver?

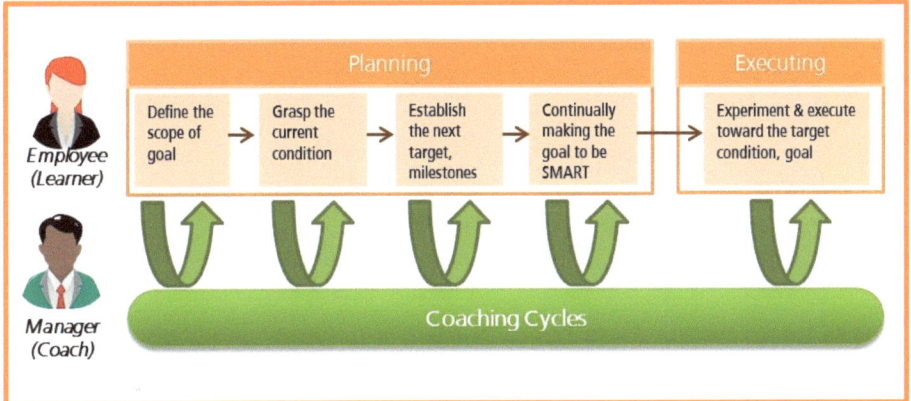

Topic 7: Infographics 101

Infographics for your work

Your Thoughts

> *How do you design an infographic that provides impact for your courseware?*

"Design is a plan for arranging elements in such a way as best to accomplish a particular purpose." – Charles Eames

Topic 7: Infographics 101

How Can We Create Engaging Infographics?

1. Choose a story for the infographic

In every set of data, there's a story. Before you start creating your infographic, think of the story you are trying to tell. The angle you choose will help you determine which information to include.

Two approaches

Data-driven – when you already possess data, and you want to tell the story based on your data. In essence, you use the data to drive the storyline.

Problem/Question – where you need to analyze the problem you that you are trying to answer with your story. In this approach, you need to put yourself in your audience shoes to reveal a compelling story angle that has the following properties::

- Solves a problem
- Provides useful and practical answers, tips
- Reframes conventional questions
- Challenges popular beliefs or status quo
- Provides unconventional answer to common question

Topic 7: Infographics 101

How Can We Create Engaging Infographics?

2. Select a type of Infographic to visualize your story

There are several types of infographic format and layout. Here are the most common types that you may choose from:

Type	Description	Example
Statistical	shows a summary or overview of data with one or more graphs, tables or lists.	
Timeline (time-oriented)	shows progress of information over a chronological time period.	
Process driven	demonstrates a linear or branching process as a how to, teaches the workings of an object or flow chart showing choices in a decision process	
Informational	are most likely a poster that summarizes topic with some extra bits of information.	

Topic 7: Infographics 101

How Can We Create Engaging Infographics?

2. Select a type of Infographic to visualize your story

Type	Description	Example
Geographic	displays data with location map.	
Compare/ contrast	illustrates notable similarities or differences as a "this versus that" infographic or as a table or simple list.	
Hierarchical	demonstrates a chart with levels.	
Research-based	similar to the statistical infographic, but based on research. Can be used to compare unlike items with popular sets of data.	

Topic 7: Infographics 101

How Can We Create Engaging Infographics?

3. Gather the relevant data

There are three approaches to using your data to make an infographic.

Use your data – if you apply the data-driven approach to infographics, you are probably using your own data. Alternatively, your organisation might have data on the subject or story that you want to write.

Original research – Nothing beats original research. You don't require a research team or a data scientist for this task. You can conduct your survey research with a tool such as Survey Monkey or Google Forms.

Data source – there are plenty of public and private information sources. Here are some examples:
- Data. Gov
- UN data
- Google Public Data
- World Bank
- World Economic Forum
- Statista
- Government statutory board (Published data)

Topic 7: Infographics 101

How Can We Create Engaging Infographics?

4. Design the infographic

Once you have got the story, the type of infographic and the data. Now you have to put them all together into an attractive looking infographic.

> **Tips:**
> - Go to Pinterest and search for "Infographics".
> - Go to the Templates page of Canva
> - Choose one or two that you prefer. Then use that as the base style.
> - Sketch on paper an outline of the infographic with the main components such as charts and elements
> - Build the infographic using a tool such as Canva (using the framework and template)
> - Change the colour, fonts and other elements to create your style derivative.

Topic 7: Infographics 101

How Can We Create Engaging Infographics?

4. Design the infographic

Some design elements are essential during the design process. Here are the major elements involved:

- Chart Types to be used:
- Typography:
- Photography:
- Colour Schemes:
- Contrasting Colour, imagery
- Balance (Symmetrical and Asymmetrical)
- Consistency of the design elements used (flow and using the same style)
- Negative Space (white spaces)

Topic 7: Infographics 101

How Can We Create Engaging Infographics?

4. Design the infographic

Designing Hacks

Content outline:
Before you start creating the infographic, it would be wise to create an outline on paper as it helps you to organize the flow of the story.

Colour scheme:
The best way to select an appropriate colour scheme is to browse at what other infographics have to source for inspiration.

Layout:
Choose a layout. Stick to a simple grid for symmetry and orientation that gives high readability. Uneven margins disrupt the information and forms barriers to the audience. Hence, the infographic should be well balanced.

Font:
Use not more than two types of the fonts. Stick to a single type of font – e.g. Sans Serif types or Serif type fonts, for consistency.

Chart types:
Choose simple charts – such as those from Excel spreadsheet (bar, column, line, doughnut, pie or bubble charts.) Focus on illustrating the story point instead of making the audience to interpret the data.

Topic 7: Infographics 101

How Can We Create Engaging Infographics?

5. Integrate in your ID work

How do we integrate infographics designed in ID process?

- Align infographic as summary / overview of course content
- Can be used as a learning activity (recall / memory)
- Invoke learning discussion between subject matter expert, the content developer and instructional designer.
- Can be designed for chapter/ topical summary
- Promote your expertise (as a CV infographic)

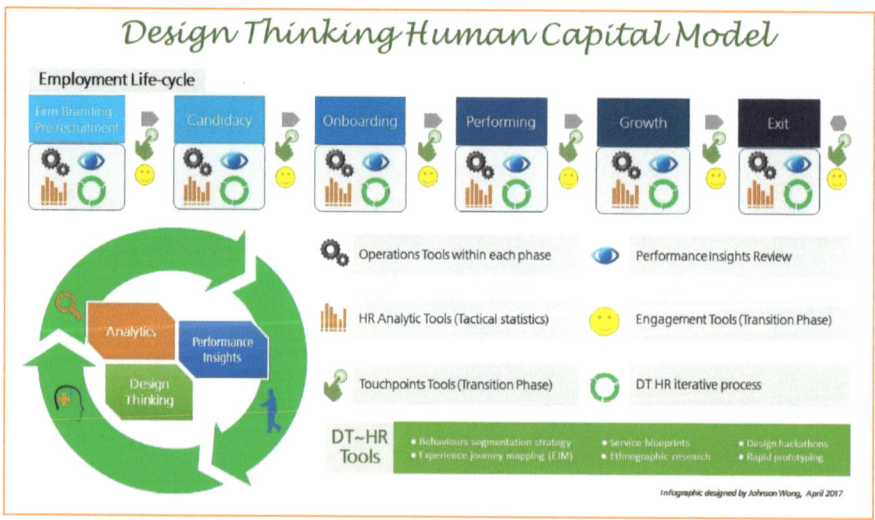

Designing infographics take time and practice, lots of practice. The next few pages provide some resources for reference.

Practice

Let's draft planning of an infographic.

Hint*: Use the basic 5 steps for creating infographic as guide.

Select the theme of your infographic which is the story.

Research and gather the information needed.

Next, write a draft script for the annotations needed.

Choose infographic layout type and design that fits the theme

Sketch the infographic and placements (placeholders if graphic or diagram is not available).

Get someone to comment the draft design and make improvements.

Topic 7: Infographics 101

Tools Available

Some useful applications with user-friendly interfaces (most of them are online graphic design platform) for creating impactful infographics are:

- Canva
- Pikotchart
- Visme
- Easel.ly
- Venngage
- MS PowerPoint
- MS Publisher
- Adobe Illustrator

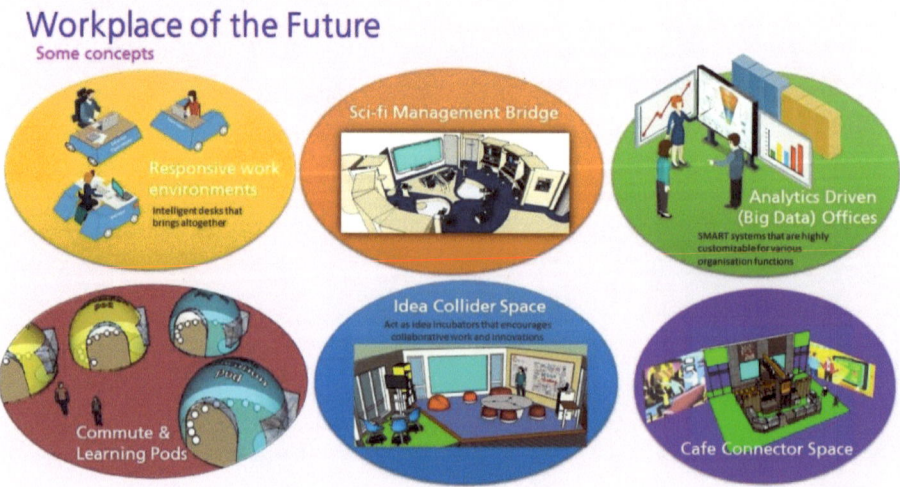

Topic 7: Infographics 101

Infographics

Your Thoughts

> *Are you getting more confident in creating infographics? How to improve my infographics?*

"Design is not just what it looks like and feels like. Design is how it works." – Steve Jobs

Topic 7: Infographics 101

Invaluable Resources and Hacks

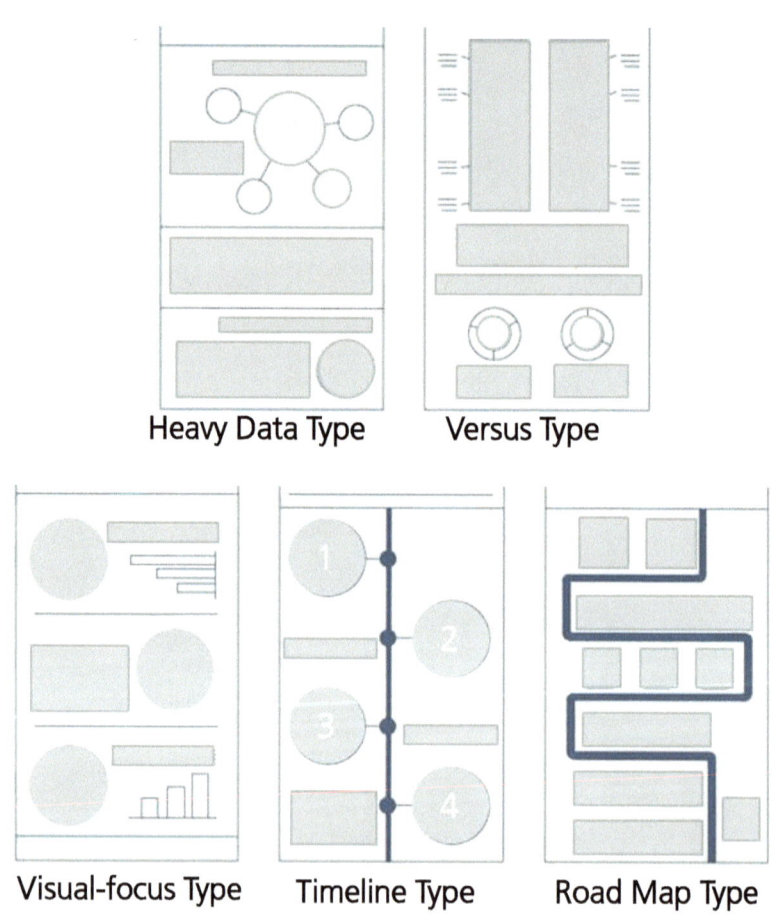

Topic 7: Infographics 101

Invaluable Resources and Hacks

Get inspirations from:

- Department of Statistics (http://www.singstat.gov.sg/)

- Pinterest (https://www.pinterest.com/)

- Flipboard (https://flipboard.com/)

- Daily infographic (http://www.dailyinfographic.com/)

- Google image search for infographics

Practice

Let's do a simple infographic based on the following data provide.

Hint*: Use the basic 5 steps and address the design elements of infographic.

Fast Facts From Modernising Learning That Delivering Results

Study participants:
- **500** L&D professionals provided detailed input to the study – up **42%** since 2013
- **29** industries (**64%** private sector; **21%** public sector; **15%** not-for-profits)
- **30** countries represented
- **3,000+** learners

Modernising learning strategy – progress update:
Expectations to deliver modernised learning strategy are rising:
- **81%** of L&D frontrunners want to respond faster to change
- **83%** want to speed up application of learning at work
- **95%** want to improve talent and performance management
- **88%** want to boost on the job productivity

The role of technology in learning for L&D perspective:
- **10%** of training budget is being allocated to learning technologies, but only **19%** of formal learning is technology-enabled
- **49%** of conformity training is technology-enabled, and the average completion rate is **65%**.
- **30%** investigating MOOCs in corporate learning

Topic 7: Infographics 101

Invaluable Resources and Hacks

Here are some examples of infographic by Johnson Wong

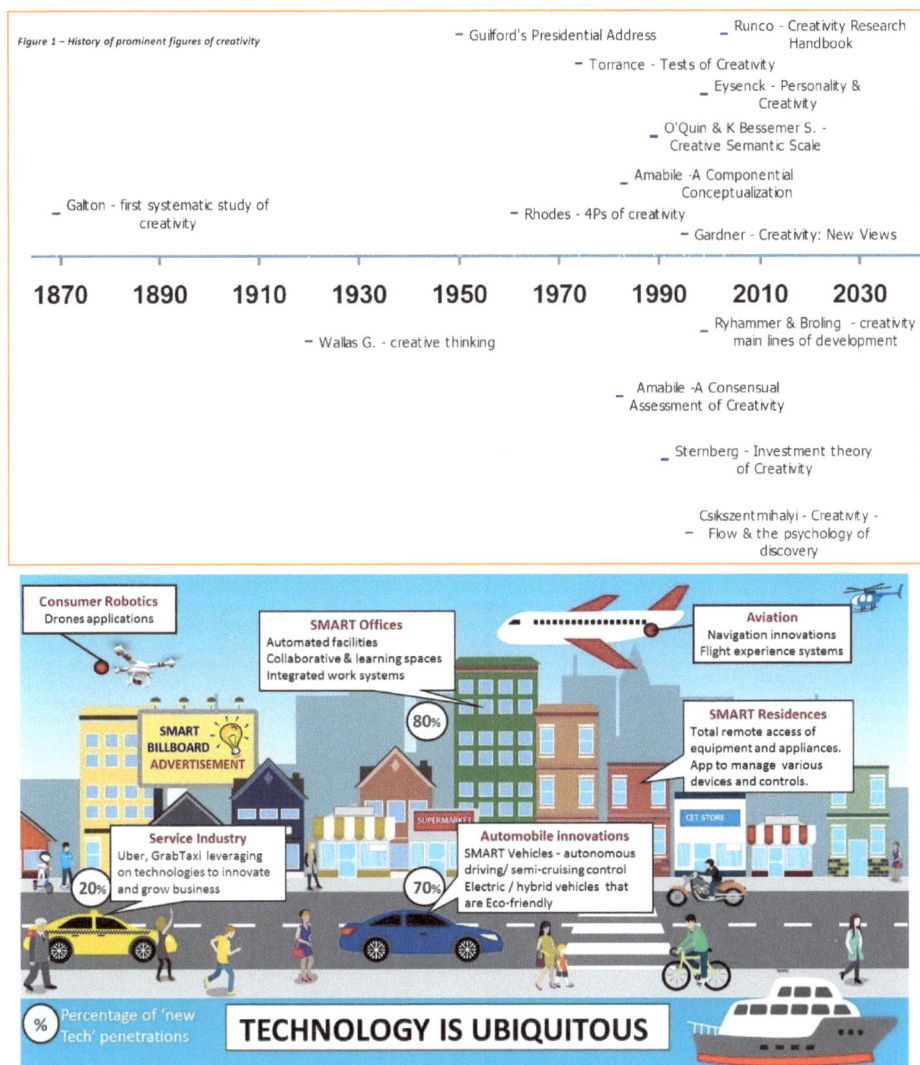

Topic 7: Infographics 101

Invaluable Resources and Hacks

Here are some examples of infographic by Johnson Wong

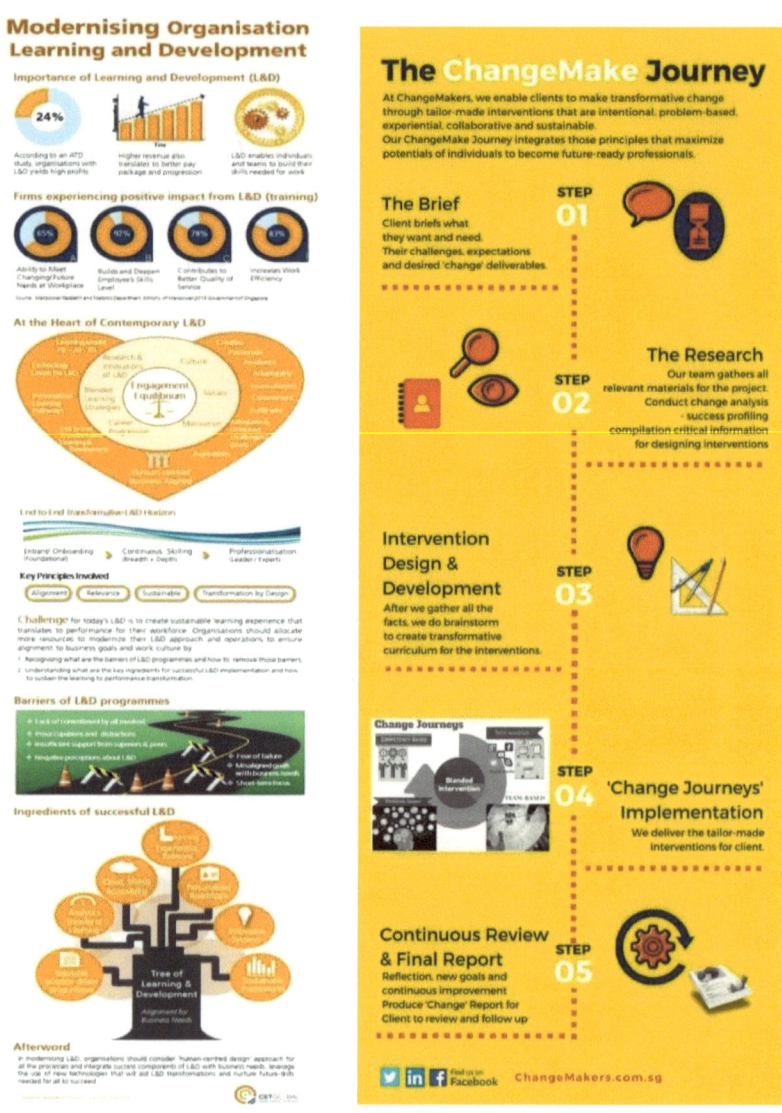

TOPIC 8
MOVING FROM STATIC CONTENT TO INTERACTIVE EXPERIENCE

Leverage on the Use of Multimedia, New Media Content
- Storyboards
- Audio Narration Tools
- Animation Tools
- Integrating Multimedia Elements
- Gamification (Introductory)

Topic 8: Moving from Static Content to Interactive Experience

Leverage on the Use of Multimedia, New Media Content

In today's forefront of learning and development, content has been readily available in digital format with interactive elements that are aimed to provide cutting-edge learning innovations.

Content are not longer static in print format, rather, they are becoming dynamically digital that is used for blended learning – in the context of this guide – we focus on some elements that are used for – e-learning.

Hence, transforming a static content for e-learning is not just merely digitalizing them for 'page turners' integrate with other multimedia elements that produce a productive learning experience.

Some of these elements are:

- Storyboards
- Audio narration tools
- Animation tools
- Integrating multimedia elements

Topic 8: Moving from Static Content to Interactive Experience

Integrating Multimedia Elements

Storyboarding for E-learning

Why is there a need?
A storyboard is crucial because it offers a map of your design. It includes all the essential information for developing the e-learning project. An excellent storyboard provides a useful guide to the development process as well as a documentation record for post-production management.

How to do storyboarding?
- Choose a storyboarding model
- Use of pre-defined templates
- Use techniques for presenting storyboard content:
    - ❏ Storytelling approach
    - ❏ Scenario-based approach
    - ❏ Toolkit approach
    - ❏ Demo-practice based approach

Other resource
http://www.learndash.com/8-easy-steps-for-elearning-storyboards

Topic 8: Moving from Static Content to Interactive Experience

Integrating Multimedia Elements

A storyboarding process model

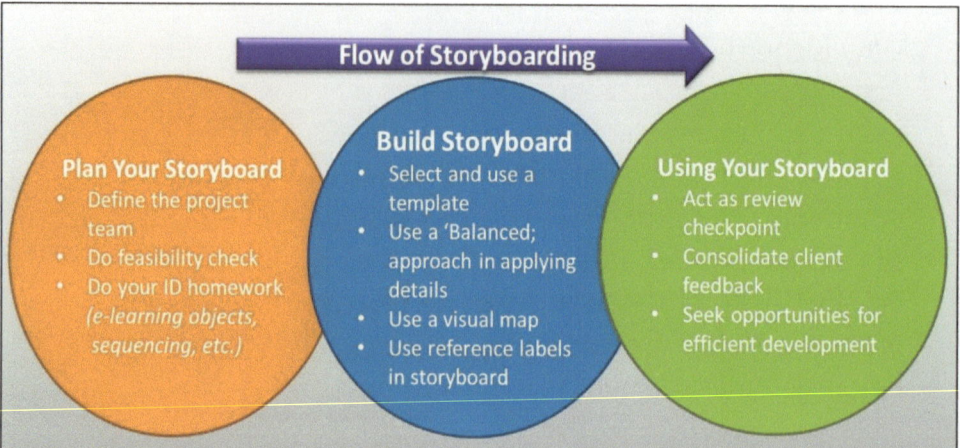

Storyboarding template:

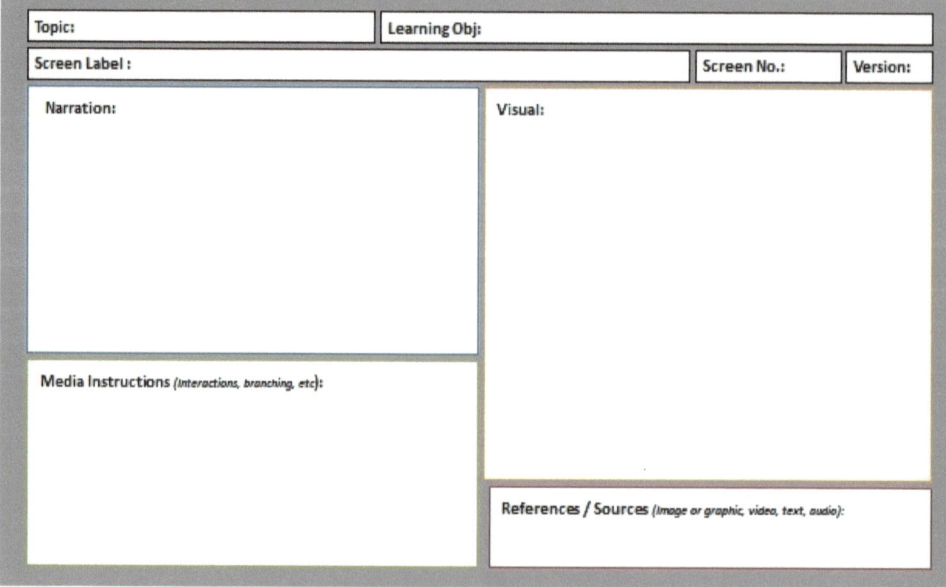

Practice

Let's do a simple storyboard exercise.

Hint*: Use a timeline –based storyboarding technique to build your story sequence.

Choose a sub-topic of particular scenario or making a definition of a process.

Use the template below to create the storyboard sequence.

Get someone to comment on your storyboard's sufficiency, quality and clarity. Make adjustments and improve your storyboarding technique.

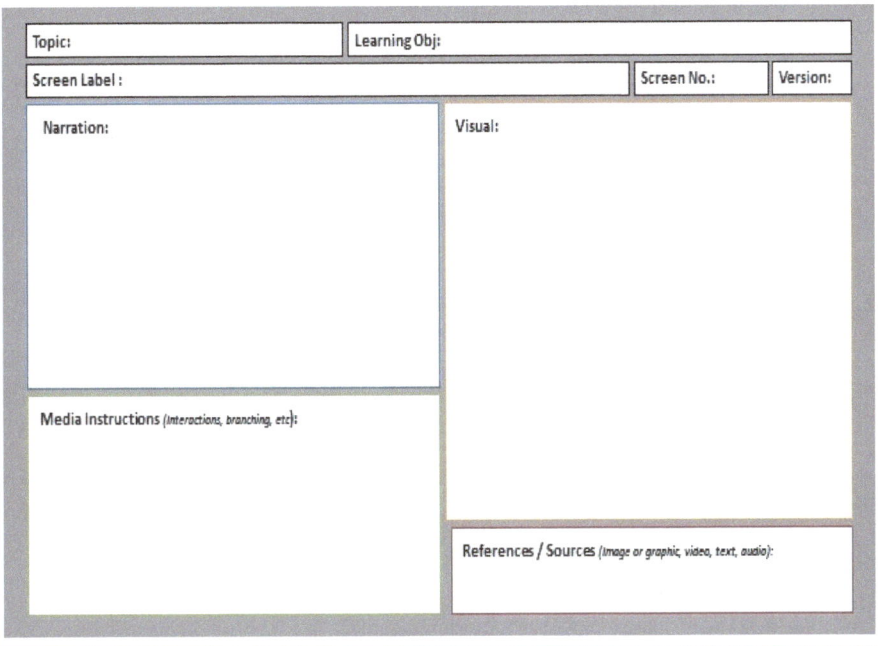

Topic 8: Moving from Static Content to Interactive Experience

Integrating Multimedia Elements

Storyboarding templates available:

- E-learning Heroes

    https://community.articulate.com/downloads/course-design/storyboards

- elearning brothers

    https://library.elearningbrothers.com/product/19388-ELB-ID-Template/?utm_campaign=elearningindustry.com&utm_source=%2Ffree-storyboard-templates-for-elearning&utm_medium=link

- elearning coach

    http://theelearningcoach.com/resources/storyboard-depot/

Topic 8: Moving from Static Content to Interactive Experience

Audio Narration Tools

- Adding the audio element is increasingly popular for e-learning courseware. The audio element used for:
    - ❑ Narrating a certain complex concept (usually paired with suitable visuals),
    - ❑ Paraphrasing (audio summarizes the on-screen text),
    - ❑ Explaining a set of instructions for a learning activity,
    - ❑ Verbatim dialogues with voice over actors (Avatars) that creates the scenario for learning (captions for each scene),
- Always use high-quality audio that is clear and concise.
- Enhance the experience with suitable background music that is not interrupting.
- Captions on dialogues, learning sequence and instructions should be available.
- Narration is usually needs to be scripted (e.g. in a storyboard for the course development)

Topic 8: Moving from Static Content to Interactive Experience

Audio Narration Tools

- Three ways to narrate your course include:
    - ❑ Hire a professional narrator
    - ❑ Use 'Text-to-Voice' application software
    - ❑ Yourself to be the narrator

- Besides narration part of creating "the voice", you may need to consider the following individuals to be involved in the recording process:
    - ❑ A scriptwriter
    - ❑ A producer (someone who has the technical skills to manage the actual sound recording activities)

Topic 8: Moving from Static Content to Interactive Experience

Audio Narration Tools

Pros and Cons on using the type of narration

Type	Pros	Cons
Professional	• High quality sound recordings were done in a professional studio • Has knowledge about compression rates, "clean audio" (noiseless product) • Has a variety of consistent voicing styles, pitch, intonation. (good for dialogues)	• More expensive (they typically use a pay-per-minute model)
Yourself (Amateur)	• Less expensive than going to a professional • Adds realism and a personal touch (authentic and original)	• Lower quality (breathing, lip smacking, background noises, etc.) • Inconsistent voice styles • Can be tough to match audio quality and have the same voice talent if updates are required in the future
Text-to-voice Software	• Likely the least expensive route • Consistent quality • Consistent voicing style/intonation • Over the last few years, quality has improved, and it is now more common alternative	• May sound robotic, unemotional and fake depending on the application that is used. • Less personal

Topic 8: Moving from Static Content to Interactive Experience

Audio Narration Tools

- Narration tool (voice recording)

    http://vocaroo.com

    https://www.chirbit.com

- Recommended narration tool (If self- recording / narration is not possible)

    http://www.wordtalk.org.uk

    http://www.naturalreaders.com

Practice

Let's do a simple narration exercise.

Hint*: Use the basic 5 steps and do address the design elements of infographic.

Write a script that is a dialogue or explanation of some processes or instructions. (1/2 a page)

Choose your favorite topic
Use one of the approaches mentioned to create a digital narration.

Get someone to comment on your narration (not the content), rather the final digital output quality and clarity.

Topic 8: Moving from Static Content to Interactive Experience

Animation Tools

- Animations can inspire our inner child, but they also have the power to improve knowledge retention, engage online learners, and simplify complex concepts.
- They can be a valuable e-Learning tool that fosters an emotional connection and gets online learners excited about the eLearning (e-courseware) process.
- Why use animations in eLearning?

  - ❏ Adds humor and entertainment to el-earning experience
  - ❏ More interactive and engaging
  - ❏ Can be used fir bite-sized e-learning activity
  - ❏ Captivates learner with re-watching scenarios
  - ❏ Creates a link between characterized scenario and actual performance processes
  - ❏ A huge plus in the 'demo' applications
  - ❏ Simplifies complex ideas and tasks by using visual sequences and representations

Resource examples:
https://community.articulate.com/articles/using-animations-for-learning

Topic 8: Moving from Static Content to Interactive Experience

Animation Tools

<u>Tips for using animations in eLearning (e-courseware)</u>

- **Choose elements that evoke the right emotions or tone.** When you are designing for the serious subject matter such as dealing with biohazards or dangerous substances, a lighthearted e-learning animation will not be appropriate. Instead, you should choose a more serious animated character who demonstrates the resolving processes and the consequences of safety practices.

- **Use one elearning character (Avatar) or topic at a time.** Animations in e-learning can quickly become confusing or chaotic especially when you do not have any constraints. Do not include information that is irrelevant. Also, do not add too many moving graphics to the animation. Busy screens will only overwhelm and distract learners from the key learning points.

Topic 8: Moving from Static Content to Interactive Experience

Animation Tools

Tips for using animations in e-learning (e-courseware)

- **Encourage learners to interact with the eLearning animation.** Learners simply watch as the story unfolds and the learning can be passive. You can make the animations more interactive by asking thought-provoking questions (aligned to the learning points) and getting them to click on trigger objects or giving them control over the animation playback. The focus is on integrating the tactile elements that invite them to take a more active role during the e-learning.

- **Pair audio to visuals.** Even the most compelling and captivating visuals fall short when you do not pair them with audio such as background music or narration. Audio has the power to generate emotional ambience that engages the learner. Also, include the option for learners to view captions or subtitles that increase their knowledge retention.

Topic 8: Moving from Static Content to Interactive Experience

Animation Tools

Tips for using animations in e-learning (e-courseware)

- Apply e-learning animations to simplify complex subjects.
  A static timeline might communicate the information, but an animated timeline that features clickable objects takes it to a whole new level.

- **Provide autonomy.** Many online learners aren't going to have the time to sit through the entire animated online presentations or e-learning activities. Learners who are accessing the e-learning content on-the-job. As such, you should make it easy for them to stop, pause, rewind, and fast forward the e-learning animation at any point. If they become distracted, they can just select the pause button and then resume when they are ready. Use clear instructions at the beginning of the e-learning animation to brief them on how to operate the course navigation to give them a better learning experience.

Topic 8: Moving from Static Content to Interactive Experience

Animation Tools

- Recommended narration tools

https://goanimate.com

GoAnimate is a *cloud-based animated video software* that doesn't require any programming. It uses drag-and-drop tools, is easy, its animation features are completely customizable, has built-in characters, props, sound effects and music.

https://www.powtoon.com/

PowToon is a free online software that allows you to create professional- looking animated videos for your courses. The process is very simple, it has an easy export system for an effortless upload, and an array of tools, features, templates, and styles.

http://www.videoscribe.co/

VideoScribe is software for creating whiteboard animations automatically. Creates your own animation with no design or technical know-how

Practice

Let's do a simple 30secs animation.

Hint*: Use the basic 5 steps and do address the design elements of infographic.

Write a script that is a dialogue or explanation of a work process or a set of procedural instruction.

Choose your favorite topic
Create a storyboard and list the items needed for each frame of animation.
Select one of the mentioned animation application (Goanimate / Powtoon / Videoscribe / or others) to create a 30sec digital segment.

Get someone to comment on the animation on the clarity, sequence and whether it is a coherent 'story' that suppose to deliver a message.

Topic 8: Moving from Static Content to Interactive Experience

Integrating Multimedia Elements

Creating a coherent and engaging mix of multimedia elements requires the use of authoring applications. The following are some recommended applications that help to blend the learning package suitable for all learning management system (LMS):

http://www.ispringsolutions.com/

https://www.articulate.com

http://softchalk.com/

http://trivantis.com/

The above authoring applications provide 30 days free-trial

Topic 8: Moving from Static Content to Interactive Experience

Static Contents to Interactive Ones

Your Thoughts

In future, how would you develop static content materials into more interactive ones?

"Great things are not done by impulse, but a series of small things brought together." – Vincent Van Gogh

Topic 8: Moving from Static Content to Interactive Experience

Gamification

Gamification is the application of game-design elements and game principles in non-game contexts.
- www.wikipedia.org

Gamification is the process of applying gaming designs and concepts to learning or training scenarios to make them more engaging and entertaining for the learner. In game-based learning events, learners compete directly against one or more individuals or participate individually in an interactive experience that rewards are better learning performance.
- www.trainingindustry.com

 *Gamification is **NOT** :*

- *Simply building a game*
- *An answer for all interactivity*
- *Simply adding game elements (points and badges) to an activity and expecting it to be more engaging instantly.*
- *A design style*
- *Solution for everything*

Topic 8: Moving from Static Content to Interactive Experience

Gamification

Why gamification for ID?

Reasons for gamifying your learning materials

- ✓ Make course content more 'alive.'
- ✓ Engage learners in 'doing things' – immersion of challenging and stimulating learning scenarios.
- ✓ Learning becomes more visible with 'progress indicators' in the gamified pathway.
- ✓ Content and activities can be designed in a more relatable and contextual that promotes authenticity of the learning
- ✓ Reinforces the learning and motivation
- ✓ Encourage learners to be competitive as well as collaborative learning depending on the design of game elements.
- ✓ In a longer horizon, the benefits of gamified materials and resources for learning enables learners to broaden and deepen their expertise.

Topic 8: Moving from Static Content to Interactive Experience

Gamification

Gamification in learning involves incorporating game elements to motivate learners. Some elements are:
- Player control
- Mastery (for example, leveling up)
- Narrative
- Immediate feedback
- Social connection
- Fun
- "Scaffolded learning" with challenges that increase
- Progress indicators (for example, points/ badges/ leaderboards, also called PBLs)

A training session that integrates some or all elements can be considered a "gamified" lesson. Good combinations create sustained engagement, meeting the needs of learners and do more than just use points and levels to motivate players.

Topic 8: Moving from Static Content to Interactive Experience

Gamification

Game elements

Elements	Brief	Example
Goal	What does a player/ team have to do to WIN?	Cross the finish line Last player who has the most cards…
Challenge	What are the obstacles put in the player's way to make reaching the goal fun and exciting?	Player 1 needs to collect BBB to get to CCC but is block by Player 2 to …
Core Mechanics	What are the core actions moves does the player do to power the play of the game?	Searching for clues, analyse the situation, solving, evaluating.
Components	What parts make up the materials of the play?	Game parts – metrics, physical manipulatives, ball, etc.
Rules	What relationship define how/what a player can and cannot do during the game?	All players must start on the line …
Space	Where does the game take place and how does that space affect the game?	Game space. e.g. on a board or virtual space on the computer.

Topic 8: Moving from Static Content to Interactive Experience

Gamification

Game Activity Guide

Knowledge Type	Instructional Strategies	Elements	Activities Type
Declarative	Elaboration, Organizing, Association, Repetition	Stories, Sorting, Matching, Replayability	Matching, Collecting
Conceptual	Examples and non-examples, Attribute classification, Metaphoric devices	Matching and sorting, Experiencing the concept	Matching games
Rules-grounded	Provide examples, Role Play	Experience consequences	Board games Stimulated work tasks
Process/Procedural	Start with overview (big picture), Teach 'how' and 'why'	Software challenges, Practice	Software scenarios, Equipment simulations
Soft skills	Analogies, Role play	Social Simulator	Leadership simulation
Affective	Encourage participation, Celebrity endorsement, Set sights that success is possible	Immersion, Providing and building success, Encouragement from 'celebrity-type' or influencer figures.	Assistive (helping) games
Psychomotor	Observe, Practice	Demonstration Haptic Devices	Virtual, Simulator

Adapted source - The Gamification of Learning and Instruction Field book. Karl M.K., Lucas B. and Rich M. (2013). *The Gamification of Learning and Instruction Fieldbook*: Ideas into Practice. USA : Pfeiffer.

Topic 8: Moving from Static Content to Interactive Experience

Gamification

How to gamify?
Steps on gamifying

1. Define the learning objectives
2. Craft Big Idea (theme)
3. Storyboard the game
4. Select the game elements
5. Build the game dynamics
6. Prototype and iterate
7. Evaluate and fine tune
8. Rollout

Practice

Let's gamify a topic.

Hint*: Use simple gamifying steps as guideline

Select a topic of your learning materials that has plenty of knowledge component (concepts, process, procedures)

Choose your favorite topic
Draft an idea on how you can gamify the learning process of the topic.

Get someone to comment the draft design and make improvements on your conceptualize game for the learning.

Conclusion

Integrated strategy

The various topics present the "how to's" tools and methods for designing content materials and resources. Revisiting instructional design principles establish the foundation of learning design. It also highlights the need to implement proper sequencing strategies and the alignment of content elements with learning goals as well as embedding contextualizations.

The focus of this book is targeted at the technical aspects of designing the learning content with practical tools and methods. Those technical "know-hows" includes executing content research, referencing methods, design and formatting strategies, software application guide for the development of learning materials, the use visuals and transforming content into interactive ones.

Moving forward with practice on the applied technical 'know-hows', it is important for one to adopt an integrated strategy when designing the learning materials and resources. Always begin with the end in mind. Identify the learners' needs and the needful learning goals.
Integrate learning principles of *storytelling* when designing your materials would likely yield a more coherent and impactful learning experiences for your target audience.

References

American Psychological Association. (2010). *Publication manual of the American Psychological Association* (5th ed.). Washington, DC: Author.

Atkinson, S. (2012). *Taxonomy circles – visualisations of educational domains*. Retrieved 16 October 2016 from: https://spatkinson.wordpress.com/tag/blooms-taxonomy/.

Cranton, P. (2000). *Planning instruction for adult learners*. Wall and Emerson.

Citations in Text. (n.d.). Retrieved from 12 October 2016 from http://www.johnwiley.com.au/highered/psych2e/jcu_demo/interactive_writing/dswmed

Ertmer, P., and Quinn, J. (2002). *The ID Casebook: Case Studies in Instructional Design (2nd Edition)*. Eaglewood Cliffs, NJ: Prentice-Hall.

Google Inc. (2016). *Google Search Functions*. Retrieved 12 October 2016 from: https://support.google.com/websearch#topic=3378866.

HarvardGenerator. (2016). *Harvard Reference Style*. Retrieved 15 October 2016 from: http://www.harvardgenerator.com/.

How long does copyright last? I National Library of Australia. (n.d.). Retrieved 14 October 2016 from https://www.nla.gov.au/how-long-does-copyright-last

IPOS Intellectual Property Office of Singapore (2016). *Intellectual Property and Copyright*. Retrieved from 16 October 2016 from: http://www.ipos.gove.sg.

Rothwell, W.J., Benscoter, B., King, M., and King, S.B. (2015). *Mastering the Instructional Design Process: A Systematic Approach* (5th ed.).Pfeiffer.

Glossary

Abbreviations

ADDIE	Analyse, Design, Develop, Implement, Evaluate
AP	Assessment Plan
APA	American Psychological Association
AR	Assessment Rubric
CC	Creative Commons
CO	Course Outline
ELO	Enabling Learning Objective
ID	Instructional Design
IP	Intellectual Property
LG	Learner's Guide
LO	Learning Objectives
LP	Lesson Plan
MS	Microsoft
PBL	Problem-Based Learning
PCC	Performance, Conditions, Criteria
PPT	PowerPoint
TG	Trainer's Guide
TLO	Terminal Learning Objective
SB	Storyboard
SMART	Specific, Measureable, Achievable, Relevant, Time-bound
WSQ	Workforce Skills Qualifications

About the Author

Johnson Wong V. P.

A design-thinker and learning strategist, he has more than 15 years of experience working in learning & development field for the higher education sector and private training entities, where he has conducted numerous research studies, facilitation and training workshops in both private and public schools in Singapore.

He exemplifies lifelong learning throughout his career and has earned a diverse suite of credentials include Master of Science, Bachelor Degree in Engineering Management, Graduate Diploma in Human Resource Management, Diploma in Adult and Continuing Education, and Advanced Certificate in Training and Assessment.

At a Singapore consulting firm, he provides services for clients in learning design, learning technology solutions (e-courses) and training advisory. He is also an academic advisor at a private education institute, where he facilitates courses such as research design and human capital development & management related skills.

Other articles published

Training Journal
From learning to performance: Connecting the dots
https://www.trainingjournal.com/articles/opinion/learning-performance-connecting-dots

Critical questions for better decision making
http://www.trainingjournal.com/articles/opinion/critical-questions-better-decision-making

Training Industry
Using Critical Conversations to Raise Difficult Issues and Increase Productivity
https://www.trainingindustry.com/leadership/articles/using-critical-conversations-to-raise-difficult-issues-and-increase-productivity

Redefining the Next Lap of Human Capital: Design Thinking in Learning and Development
http://www.trainingindustry.com/articles/redefining-the-next-lap-of-human-capital-design-thinking-in-learning-and-development

HR in Asia
Managing Performance as an 'Experience-Continuum'
http://www.hrinasia.com/people-development/managing-performance-as-an-experience-continuum/